Rick Steves®

SNAPSHOT

S0-AEH-240

Lisbon

CONTENTS

INTRODUCTION

This Snapshot guide, excerpted from my guidebook *Rick Steves Portugal,* introduces you to Lisbon, the country's culturally rich capital. Here at the far western edge of Europe, prices are reasonable, the people are warm, and the pace of life slows. Wander through Lisbon's characteristic downtown neighborhoods like the hilly Alfama and the busy Baixa, then head up to the lanes of Bairro Alto at night to find a good fado bar. The grand Belém district offers a look at Lisbon's historic architecture and seafaring glory, from the 16th-century Monastery of Jerónimos to the Monument to the Discoveries. Or visit the Gulbenkian Museum, the best of Lisbon's 40 museums, offering 5,000 years' worth of art.

Day-trip to the touristy but lovely town of Sintra, dotted with the fanciful Pena Palace, royal National Palace, and evocative Moorish castle ruins atop a hill.

To help you have the best trip possible, I've included the following topics in this book:

• **Planning Your Time,** with advice on how to make the most of your limited time

• **Orientation,** including tourist information offices (abbreviated as TI), tips on public transportation, local tour options, and helpful hints

• **Sights** with ratings:

      ▲▲▲—Don't miss

      ▲▲—Try hard to see

      ▲—Worthwhile if you can make it

      No rating—Worth knowing about

• **Sleeping** and **Eating,** with good-value recommendations in every price range

• **Connections,** with tips on trains, buses, and driving

Practicalities, near the end of this book, has information on money, staying connected, transportation, lodging, restaurants, and more, plus Portuguese survival phrases.

To travel smartly, read this little book in its entirety before you go. It's my hope that this guide will make your trip more meaningful and rewarding. Traveling like a temporary local, you'll get the absolute most out of every mile, minute, and dollar.

Boa-viagem!

Rick Steves

LISBON

Lisboa

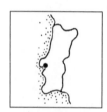

Lisbon is ramshackle, trendy, and charming all at once—an endearing mix of now and then. Vintage trolleys shiver up and down its hills, bird-stained statues mark grand squares, taxis rattle and screech through cobbled lanes, and Art Nouveau cafés are filled equally with well-worn and well-dressed locals—nursing their coffees side-by-side. It's a city of proud ironwork balconies, multicolored tiles, and mosaic sidewalks; of bougainvillea and red-tiled roofs with antique TV antennas; and of foodie haunts and designer boutiques.

Lisbon, Portugal's capital, is the country's banking and manufacturing center. Residents call their city Lisboa (leezh-BOH-ah), which comes from the Phoenician *Alis Ubbo,* meaning "calm port." A port city on the yawning mouth of the Rio Tejo (REE-oo TAY-zhoo—the Tagus River), Lisbon welcomes large ships to its waters and state-of-the-art dry docks. And more recently, it has become a hugely popular stop with cruise ships.

Romans (2nd century B.C.) and Moors (8th century) were the earliest settlers in Lisbon, but the city's glory days were in the 15th and 16th centuries, when explorers such as Vasco da Gama opened new trade routes around Africa to India, making Lisbon one of Europe's richest cities. Portugal's Age of Discovery fueled rapid economic growth, which sparked the flamboyant art boom called the Manueline period—named for King Manuel I (r. 1495-1521).

On the morning of All Saints' Day in 1755, a tremendous earthquake hit Lisbon, followed by a devastating tsunami and days of fires. (For more on this cataclysmic event, see page 38.) Chief Minister Marquês de Pombal rebuilt downtown Lisbon on a grid plan, with broad boulevards and generous squares. It's this

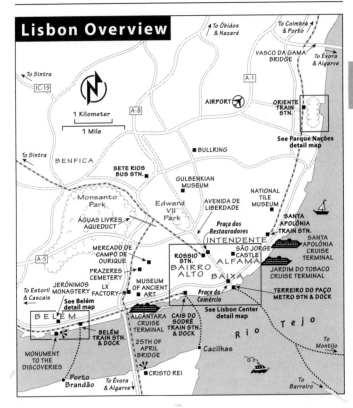

"Pombaline"-era neighborhood where you'll spend much of your time, though remnants of Lisbon's preearthquake charm survive in Belém, the Alfama, and the Bairro Alto district. The bulk of your sightseeing will likely be in these neighborhoods.

As the Paris of the Portuguese-speaking world, Lisbon (pop. 548,000 in the core) is the Old World capital of its former empire—some 100 million people stretching from Europe to Brazil to Africa to China. Portugal remains on largely good terms with its former colonies—and immigrants from places such as Mozambique and Angola add diversity and flavor to the city, making it as likely that you'll hear African music as much as Portuguese fado.

With its characteristic hills, trolleys, famous suspension bridge, and rolling fog, Lisbon has a San Francisco feel. Enjoy all this world-class city has to offer: elegant outdoor cafés, exciting art, fun-to-browse shops, stunning vistas, delicious food, entertaining museums, and a salty sailors' quarter with a hill-capping castle.

PLANNING YOUR TIME

Lisbon merits at least three days, including a day for a side-trip to Sintra. If you have more time, there's plenty to do.

Day 1: Get oriented to Lisbon's three downtown neighborhoods (following my three self-guided walks; see page 24): Alfama, Baixa, and Bairro Alto/Chiado. Start where the city did, at its castle (hop a taxi or Uber to get there at 9:00, before the crowds hit). After surveying the city from the highest viewpoint in town, walk downhill into the characteristic Alfama neighborhood and end at the Fado Museum. From there, zip over to the big main square (Praça do Comércio) to explore the Baixa, then ride up the Elevador da Glória funicular to begin the Bairro Alto and Chiado walk. Art lovers can then hop a taxi to the Gulbenkian Museum (open until 18:00, closed Tue), while shoppers can browse the boutiques of the Chiado and Príncipe Real. Consider dinner at a fado show in the Bairro Alto or the Alfama. For more evening options, see "Entertainment in Lisbon" (page 92).

Day 2: Trolley to Belém and tour the monastery, tower, and National Coach Museum. Have lunch in Belém, then tour the Museum of Ancient Art on your way back to Lisbon.

Day 3: Side-trip to Sintra to tour the Pena Palace and explore the ruined Moorish castle.

More Time: An extra day (or more) lets you slow down and relax—potentially spreading the "Day 1" activities over two days. Use the extra time to explore and window-shop characteristic neighborhoods and nurse drinks bought from kiosks on relaxing squares. You could also head to the Parque das Nações and/or National Tile Museum, or take a food tour.

Monday Options: Many top sights are closed on Monday, particularly in Belém. That'd be a good day to choose among the following options: Take my self-guided neighborhood walks; day-trip to Sintra (where all of the major sights are open); go on a guided walking tour with Lisbon Walker or Inside Lisbon (see page 19); or head to Parque das Nações for a dose of modern Lisbon.

Orientation to Lisbon

LISBON: A VERBAL MAP

Greater Lisbon has close to three million people and intimidating sprawl. But most visitors spend virtually all their time in the old city center, a delightful series of parks, boulevards, and squares in a crusty, well-preserved architectural shell. But on even a brief visit, you'll also want to venture to Belém, the riverfront suburb with many top sights.

Here's an overview of the city's layout:

Baixa (Lower Town): Downtown Lisbon fills a valley flanked by two hills along the banks of the Rio Tejo. In that valley the neighborhood called Baixa (BYE-shah), stretches from the main squares—Rossio (roh-SEE-oo) and Praça da Figueira (PRAH-sah dah fee-GAY-rah)—to the waterfront. The Baixa is a flat, pleasant shopping area of grid-patterned streets. As Lisbon's main crossroads and transportation hub, touristy Baixa has lots of hotels, venerable cafés and pastry shops, and kitschy souvenir stands.

Alfama: The hill to the east of the Baixa is the Alfama (al-FAH-mah), a colorful tangle of medieval streets, topped by São Jorge Castle. The lower slopes of the Alfama are a spilled spaghetti of old sailors' homes.

Bairro Alto (High Town): The hill to the west of the Baixa is capped by the Bairro Alto (BYE-roh AHL-too), with a tight grid of steep, narrow, and characteristic lanes. Downhill toward the Baixa, the Bairro Alto fades into the trendy and inviting **Chiado** (shee-AH-doo), with linger-a-while squares, upmarket restaurants, and high-fashion stores.

Modern Lisbon: From this historic core, the modern city stretches north (sloping uphill) along wide Avenida da Liberdade and beyond (way beyond), where you find Edward VII Park, the Gulbenkian Museum, breezy botanical gardens, the bullring, and the airport.

Away from the Center: Along the riverfront are two worthwhile areas. Three miles west of the center is the suburb of **Belém** (beh-LAYNG), home to much of Lisbon's best sightseeing, with several Age of Discovery sights (particularly the Monastery of Jerónimos)—and you can visit the Museum of Ancient Art along the way. Five miles north of the center is **Parque das Nações,** site of the Expo '98 world's fair and now a modern shopping complex and riverfront promenade (the National Tile Museum is about halfway there).

Few tourists venture **across the Rio Tejo,** but public ferries sail to the little port communities of Cacilhas (from downtown; connected by bus to the towering Cristo Rei statue) or Porto Brandão (from Belém)—both have popular fish restaurants.

TOURIST INFORMATION

Lisbon has several tourist offices—all branded "ask me L¿sboa"—and additional information kiosks sprout around town during the busy summer months (www.visitlisboa.com). The main TIs are strategically located on **Praça dos Restauradores** at Palácio Foz (daily 9:00-20:00, tel. 213-463-314; TI for rest of Portugal in same office; there's also a kiosk across the street); on **Praça do Comércio** (two locations; both daily 10:00-20:00, tel. 210-312-810); and at the **airport** (daily 7:00-24:00, tel. 218-450-660). Smaller TI kiosks are at the bottom (south end) of **Rossio** (daily 10:00-13:00

LISBON

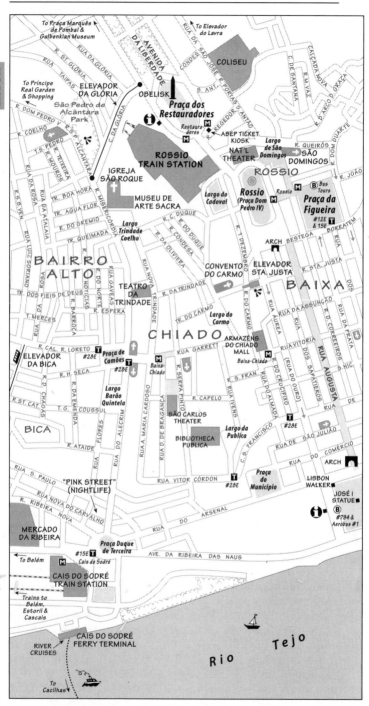

LISBON

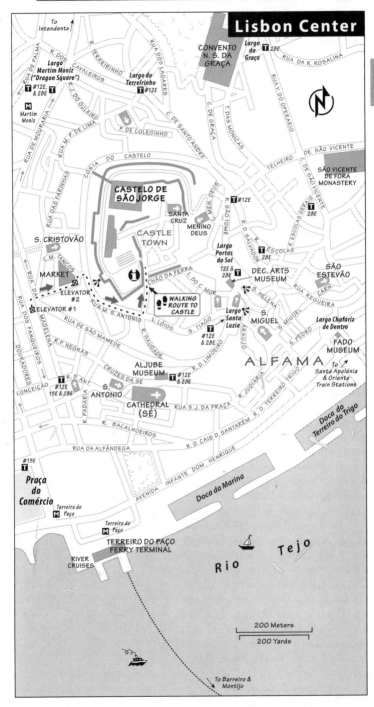

& 14:00-18:00, mobile 910-517-914); across the street from the monastery in **Belém** (Tue-Sat 10:00-13:00 & 14:00-18:00, closed Sun-Mon, tel. 213-658-435); at **Parque das Nações**, in front of the Vasco da Gama mall toward the riverfront (daily 10:00-13:00 & 14:00-19:00, Oct-March until 18:00); and inside **Santa Apolónia train station** (open only Tue-Sat 7:00-9:00, closed Sun-Mon, toward the end of track 3). At any TI, you can buy a LisboaCard (see next) and pick up the free city map and information-packed *Follow Me Lisboa* booklet (monthly, cultural and museum listings—also available at www.visitlisboa.com, "Publications" tab).

LisboaCard: This card covers all public transportation (as well as trains to Sintra and Cascais) and free entry to many museums (including the Museum of Ancient Art, National Tile Museum, National Coach Museum, Monastery of Jerónimos, and Belém Tower). It also provides discounts on many museums (including sights at Sintra), city tours, and river cruises. You can buy the card at Lisbon's TIs (including the airport TI), but not at participating sights. If you plan to museum-hop, the card is a good value, particularly for a day in Belém (covers your transportation and most sightseeing). The card is unnecessary if you're a student or senior, for whom most sights are free or half-price. When considering the card, remember that many sights are closed on Monday and free on the first Sunday of each month. Carry the LisboaCard booklet with you—some discounts require coupons contained inside (€19/24 hours, €32/48 hours, €39/72 hours, kids 5-11 nearly half-price, includes excellent explanatory guidebook, www.askmelisboa.com).

ARRIVAL IN LISBON

For complete information on arriving at or departing from Lisbon, see "Lisbon Connections" at the end of this chapter.

By Plane: International and domestic flights arrive at Lisbon's Portela Airport. On arrival, check in at the handy TI—it's a smart place to buy your LisboaCard. Options for getting into town include taxis, Uber, Aerobus, or Metro (all described on page 121).

By Train: Lisbon has four primary train stations: Santa Apolónia (to Spain and most points north), Oriente (for the Algarve, Évora, Sintra, and fast trains to the north), Rossio (for Sintra, Óbidos, and Nazaré), and Cais do Sodré (for coastal Belém, Estoril, and Cascais). For schedules, see www.cp.pt.

By Car: It makes absolutely no sense to drive in Lisbon. Dump your rental car at the airport and connect to your hotel by a €10 taxi or Uber ride (car return clearly marked; the airport is also a good place to pick up a car on your way out of town).

If you must drive and are entering Lisbon from the north, a series of boulevards takes you into the center. Navigate by following signs to *Centro, Avenida da República, Marquês de Pombal, Avenida da Liberdade, Praça dos Restauradores, Rossio,* and *Praça do Comércio.* If coming from the east over the Vasco da Gama Bridge and heading for the airport, take the first exit after the bridge.

Parking: There are many safe underground pay parking lots in Lisbon (follow blue *P* signs), but they discourage anything but short stays by getting more expensive by the hour. Expect to pay €20 per day (the most central Praça dos Restauradores costs €17.50/24 hours if you pay when you arrive).

HELPFUL HINTS

Exchange Rate: €1 = about $1.10

Country Calling Code: 351 (see page 150 for dialing instructions)

Theft Alert: Lisbon has piles of people doing illegal business on the street. While the city is generally safe, if you're looking for trouble—especially after dark—you may find it.

Pickpockets target tourists on the trolleys, elevators, and funiculars. Enjoy the sightseeing, but be aware. Wear your money belt and keep your pack zipped up. Some thieves pose as tourists by wearing cameras and toting maps. Be on guard whenever you're in a crush of people, or jostled as you enter or leave a tram or bus. And be wary of beggars in the street— some are scammers and pickpockets.

Pedestrian Warning: Lisbon's unique black-and-white pattered tile pavement, while picturesque, can be very slippery. And trams can be quiet and sneak up on you if you're not paying attention. Even some of the tuk-tuks are "eco" (electric) and can zip up behind you silently.

Free Days and Monday Closures: National museums are free on the first Sunday of each month (all day or until 14:00); the (private) Gulbenkian Museum is free every Sunday after 14:00. Many major sights are closed on Monday, including Lisbon's Museum of Ancient Art, National Tile Museum, and Fado Museum, as well as Belém's Monastery of Jerónimos, Coach Museum, and Belém Tower.

Market Days: Tuesdays and Saturdays are flea- and food-market days in the Alfama's Campo de Santa Clara. On Sundays, the LxFactory zone, in the shadow of the 25th of April Bridge, hosts a lively farmers market (9:30-16:00; for location, see "Lisbon Overview" map).

Useful App: ∩ For a free audio tour that covers portions of my self-guided walks in this book, get the **Rick Steves' Audio Europe** app (for details, see page 155).

Post Office: Modern, user-friendly post offices (*correios* or *CTT*) are at Praça dos Restauradores 58 (closed Sun) and on Rua da Santa Justa 15 (closed Sat-Sun).

Laundry: Drop off clothes at centrally located **5àSec Lavandaria** (€7.50/kilo, same-day wash-and-dry service usually possible if you drop off early, Mon-Fri 8:00-20:00, Sat 10:00-20:00, closed Sun, next to the bottom level of the Armazéns do Chiado mall and lower entrance to Baixa-Chiado Metro stop at Rua do Crucifixo 99, tel. 213-479-599).

Travel Agency: **GeoStar** is handy and helpful for train tickets (Portugal only) and flights (Mon-Fri 9:30-18:30, closed Sat-Sun, Praça dos Restauradores 14, tel. 213-245-240).

Ticket Kiosk: The green **ABEP kiosk** at the bottom end of Praça dos Restauradores is a handy spot to buy a city transit pass, LisboaCard, and tickets to bullfights, soccer games, concerts, and other events (daily 9:00-20:00, across from TI).

GETTING AROUND LISBON

If you have a LisboaCard, you can use it to ride Lisbon's public transit (see next page). Otherwise, you'll have to buy tickets.

Ticket Options: Transit tickets are issued on a scannable **Viva Viagem** card, which works on the Metro, funiculars, trolleys, buses, Santa Justa elevator, and some short-distance trains. The card itself costs €0.50 and is reloadable, but it's not shareable—each rider needs one. You can buy or reload the card at ticket windows or machines in Metro stations (touch "without a reusable card" for first-time users, or "with a reusable card" to top up). Keep your Viva Viagem card handy—you'll need to place it on the magnetic pad when entering and leaving the system.

You can use the Viva Viagem in three ways:

1. A **single-ride ticket** costs €1.40 (good for one hour of travel within Zone 1). But if you're taking even a few rides, "zapping" is a much better deal (see below).

2. A **24-hour pass** costs €6 (this version does not cover trains). If you're side-tripping to Sintra or Cascais, consider the €10 version, which includes trains to those towns (but does not include the bus at Sintra). Skip the €9 version of the 24-hour pass, which adds the ferry across the Tejo to Cacilhas (it's cheaper to simply buy separately).

3. **"Zapping"** lets you preload the card with anywhere from €3 to €40, and lowers the per-ride cost to €1.25. Figure out how much you'll need, and load it up (estimate conservatively—you can always top up later, but leftover credit is nonrefundable). If you'll be taking fewer than five rides in one day, zapping is your best deal

(and it's fun to say). Unlike the €6 24-hour pass, zapping can be used for trains to Sintra and Cascais.

Although it's possible to **pay the driver** as you board buses (€1.80), trolleys (€2.85), funiculars (€3.60), and the Santa Justa elevator (€5), only suckers do that. It's much cheaper if you get comfortable zapping with Viva Viagem.

For transit information, see www.carris.pt.

By Metro

Lisbon's simple, fast, and color-coded subway system is a delight to use (runs daily 6:30-1:00 in the morning). Though it's not nec-

 essary for getting around the historic downtown, the Metro is handy for trips to or from Rossio (M: Rossio or Restauradores), Praça do Comércio (M: Terreiro do Paço), the Gulben-kian Museum (M: São Sebastião), the Chiado neighborhood (M: Baixa-Chiado), Parque das Nações and the Oriente train station (both at M: Oriente), Sete Rios bus and train stations (M: Jardim Zoológico), and the airport (M: Aeroporto). Metro stops are marked above ground with a red "M." *Saída* means "exit." You can find a Metro map at any Metro stop, on most city maps, and on the Metro website (www.metrolisboa.pt).

By Trolley, Funicular, and Bus

Lisbon's buses are fine, but for fun and practical public transportation, use the trolleys and funiculars. These are cheapest zapping with a Viva Viagem card (see above for ticketing options).

Like San Francisco, Lisbon sees its classic **trolleys** as part of its heritage, and has kept a few in use: Trolleys #12E (circling the Alfama) and #28E (a scenic ride across the old town) use vintage cars; #15E (to Belém) uses a modern, air-conditioned version. Buy a ticket, have a pass, validate your Viva Viagem card as you enter... or risk a big fine on the spot. Please be mindful of locals—especially little old Alfama ladies—who need a seat. Trolleys rattle by every 10 minutes or so (or every 15-20 minutes after 19:00) and run until about 23:00. For much more on using and enjoying Lisbon's delightful trolleys, see page 14.

By Taxi or Uber

Lisbon is a great taxi town except at the airport and cruise terminals, which attract greedy cabbies (for tips on dodging their scams, see "Lisbon Connections"). Otherwise, especially if you're with a companion, Lisbon's cabs are a cheap time-saver. Rides start at €4,

LISBON

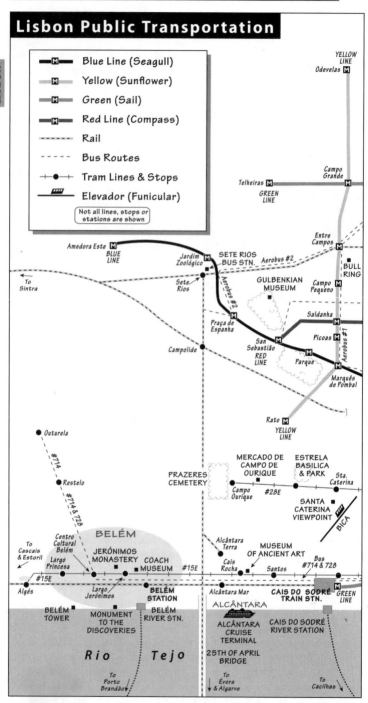

Lisbon Public Transportation

Legend:
- **M**━ Blue Line (Seagull)
- **M**━ Yellow (Sunflower)
- **M**━ Green (Sail)
- **M**━ Red Line (Compass)
- ⋯⋯ Rail
- ---- Bus Routes
- +━●━+ Tram Lines & Stops
- ▰ Elevador (Funicular)

Not all lines, stops or stations are shown

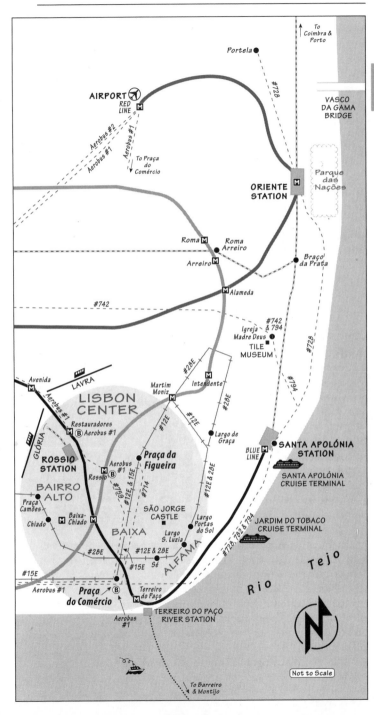

and you can go anywhere in the center for around €6. Decals on the window clearly spell out all charges in English. Be sure your driver turns on the meter; it should start at about €4 and be set to *Tarifa 1* (Mon-Fri 6:00-21:00, including the airport) or *Tarifa 2* (same drop rate, a little more per kilometer; for nights, weekends, and holidays). If the meter reads *Tarifa 3, 4,* or *5,* simply ask the cabbie to change it, unless you're going to Belém, which is considered outside the city limits.

Cabs are generally easy to hail on the street (green light means available, lit number on the roof indicates it's taken). If you're having a hard time flagging one down, ask a passerby for the location of the nearest taxi stand: *praça de taxi* (PRAH-sah duh taxi). They're all over the town center.

Lisbon is also an excellent **Uber** town. The ride-sharing app works here just like back home; it's at least as affordable as a taxi (often cheaper, except during "surge" pricing); and the drivers and their cars are generally of great quality. If you've never tried Uber abroad, do it here.

Tours in Lisbon

ON WHEELS
▲▲Trolleys

Lisbon's trolleys—many of them vintage models from the 1920s—shake and shiver through the old parts of town, somehow safely weaving within inches of parked cars, climbing steep hills, and offering sightseers breezy views of the city (rubberneck out the window and you die). As you board, swipe your Viva Viagem card (see "Getting Around Lisbon") or pay the driver (€2.85), and take a seat.

Buses and trolleys usually share the same stops and routes. Signs for bus stops list the bus number, while signs for trolley stops include an E (for *eléctrico*) before or after the route number. Remember that most pickpocketing in Lisbon takes place on trolleys, so enjoy the ride, but keep an eye on your belongings. You can think of trolleys #28E and #12E as hop-on, hop-off do-it-yourself tours (zapping tickets are good for an hour, and a 24-hour pass comes with unlimited hopping on and off).

Crowd Warning: Lisbon's trolleys are an absolute joy...*if* you're sitting down and looking out the window with the wind in your face. But if you have to stand, you won't be able to see

Lisbon's Best Viewpoints

The first three viewpoints are included in the self-guided walks described in this chapter:

- Miradouro de São Pedro de Alcântara (view terrace in Bairro Alto, at top of Elevador da Glória funicular; see "The Bairro Alto and Chiado Stroll," page 43)
- São Jorge Castle (on top of the Alfama; see photo above and "The Alfama Stroll and the Castle," page 24)
- Miradouro das Portas do Sol (south slope of Alfama; see "The Alfama Stroll and the Castle," page 24)
- Elevador de Santa Justa (in the Baixa, page 48)
- Cristo Rei (statue on hillside across the Rio Tejo, page 84)
- Edward VII Park (at north end of Avenida da Liberdade)
- Bica Miradouro (atop the Elevador da Bica funicular)

out the (low) windows, and you'll spend the jostling ride trying to steady yourself. At peak times, hordes of tourists wait at trolley stops (particularly at starting points, such as on Praça da Figueira for route #12E). My advice is, rather than being determined to take a particular trolley at a particular time, keep an eye on trolleys as they roll by...and if you see an empty one pull up, hop on and take advantage of the open space.

Trolley #28E

Trolley #28E is a San Francisco-style Lisbon joyride. In the center of town, this trolley is often extremely crowded. To enjoy a seat for the entire scenic ride, consider taking a taxi to Mercado de Campo de Ourique for a meal or to the Prazeres Cemetery (both described next) and catching the #28E from there, where it embarks on its route across town. The following are notable trolley stops from west to east:

Campo Ourique: The **Prazeres Cemetery,** at the western terminus of route #28E, is a vast park-like necropolis dense with the mausoleums of leading Lisbon families and historic figures dating back to the 19th century (daily 9:00-17:00).

Igreja Sto. Condestável: The first stop after the cemetery is next to an angular modern church. Hiding just behind the church is the **Mercado de Campo de Ourique,** a 19th-century iron-and-glass market that's now a trendy food circus (see page 113).

Estrela: Two stops later, the trolley pulls up in front of another large church (on the right). The 18th-century, late Baroque **Estrela Basilica** has stairs winding up to the roof for a view both out and down into the church (€4, daily 10:00-18:00). Across the street is the gate into **Estrela Park,** a cozy neighborhood scene with exotic plants, a pond-side café, and a playground.

Torre de Tombo: At the next stop, you'll see a garden poking up on the left behind a high wall (which hides the prime minister's residence). Next up is the huge, stately **Assembly of the Republic** building—home to Portugal's parliament. Soon after, the trolley enters a relatively narrow street at the edge of the Bairro Alto.

Santa Catarina: A couple of stops into the Bairro Alto, this area is enjoyable for a stroll through characteristic streets downhill to the **Miradouro de Santa Catarina,** a view terrace with inviting cafés and bars.

Calhariz-Bica: Keep an eye on the streets to your right. You'll spot the top of the **Elevador da Bica funicular,** which drops steeply through a rough-and-tumble neighborhood to the riverfront.

City-Center Stops: From here, the downtown stops come fast and furious—**Chiado** (at Chiado's main square, Lisbon's café meeting-place); **Baixa** (on Rua da Conceição between Augusta and Prata); **Sé** (the cathedral); **Miradouro das Portas do Sol** (the Alfama viewpoint); **Campo de Santa Clara** (flea market on Tue and Sat); and the pleasant and untouristy **Graça** district (with another excellent viewpoint).

Trolley #12E

For a colorful, 20-minute loop around the castle and the Alfama, catch trolley #12E on Praça da Figueira (departs every few minutes from the stop at corner of square closest to castle). The driver can tell you when to get out for the Miradouro das Portas do Sol viewpoint near the castle (about three-quarters of the way up the hill), or you can stay on the trolley and be dropped back where you started. Here's what you'll see on this loop ride:

Leaving Praça da Figueira, you enter **Largo de Martim Moniz**—named for a knight who died heroically while using his body as a doorjamb to leave the castle gate open, allowing his Christian Portuguese comrades to get in and capture Lisbon from the Moors in 1147. These days, this gathering point is nicknamed

"Dragon Square" for the modern sculpture erected in the middle by the local Chinese community to celebrate the Year of the Dragon.

At the next stop, on the right, is the picturesque **Centro Comercial da Mouraria,** a marketplace filled with products and aromas from around the world. The big, maroon-colored building capping the hill on the left was a Jesuit monastery until 1769, when the dictatorial Marquês de Pombal booted the pesky order out of Portugal and turned the building into the Hospital São José. Today, this is an immigrant neighborhood with lots of cheap import shops. (The trendy **Intendente** neighborhood is just up the street—see page 93.)

Turning right onto Rua de Cavaleiros, you climb through the atmospheric **Mouraria neighborhood** on a street so narrow that a single trolley track is all that fits. Notice how the colorful mix of neighbors who fill the trolley all seem to know each other. If the trolley's path is blocked and can't pass, lots of horn-honking and shouts from passengers ensue until your journey resumes. Look up the skinny side streets. Marvel at the creative parking and classic laundry scenes. This was the area given to the Moors after they were driven out of the castle and Alfama. Natives know it as the home of the legendary fado singer Maria Severa as well as modern-day singer Mariza. The majority of residents these days are immigrants from Asia, making this Lisbon's version of Chinatown and Bollywood wrapped up in one.

At the crest of the hill—at the square called **Largo Rodrigues de Freitas**—you can get out to explore, eat at a cheap restaurant (see "Eating in Lisbon," later), or follow Rua de Santa Marinha to the Campo de Santa Clara flea market (Tue and Sat).

When you see the river, you're at **Largo das Portas do Sol** (Gates of the Sun), where you'll also see the remains of one of the seven old Moorish gates of Lisbon. The driver usually announces *"castelo"* (cahzh-TAY-loo) at this point. Hop out here if you want to visit the Museum and School of Portuguese Decorative Arts (see page 30), enjoy the most scenic cup of coffee in town, explore the **Alfama,** or tour the **castle.**

The trolley continues downhill. First you'll pass (on the right) the stout building called **Aljube**—a prison built on a site dating from Roman times that, more recently, housed political opponents of Portugal's fascist dictator Salazar (now housing a museum about that regime; see page 55). Just downhill is the fortress-like **Lisbon Cathedral** (on left—see page 53). And finally you roll into the **Baixa** (grid-planned Pombaline city—get off here to take my self-guided Baixa walk—see page 33). After a few blocks, you're back where you started—Praça da Figueira.

Private Trolley Tours

Yellow Bus—the dominant local tour operator (see next)—operates a hop-on, hop-off trolley tour around Lisbon. There are two lines: Hills Tramcar Tour (€19/24 hours, red, year-round) and the shorter Castle Tramcar Tour (€12/24 hours, green, summer only). These use the same tracks and stops as the cheap, easy, and frequent public trolleys described above, but cost much more. But they may be less crowded, and they come with recorded commentary (€18, 1.5-hour tour with five stops, runs every 20 minutes June-Sept 9:15-19:00, fewer off-season).

Hop-on, Hop-off Bus Tours

Various companies operate hop-on, hop-off bus tours around Lisbon. While uninspiring and not cheap—and Lisbon's sights are compact enough to easily see on your own—these tours can be handy and run daily year-round.

Yellow Bus (www.yellowbustours.com) and **Gray Line** (www.cityrama.pt) run multiple loops through town, targeted on different sights; figure around €15 for 24 hours on one loop, or about €25 for 48-hour access to all loops. Each company also offers a dizzying array of combination tickets (trolley tours, tuk-tuks, boat trips, Segway tours, discounts to city sights, and so on). Buses depart from Praça da Figueira (buy tickets from driver). When comparing your options, note that Yellow Bus tickets include some Lisbon city transit as well (public trolleys, buses, Elevador de Santa Justa, and funiculars, but not the Metro).

Tuk-Tuks

Goofy little tuk-tuks—Indian-style, three-wheel motorcycles—have invaded Lisbon. You'll see them parked in front of tourist landmarks all over town (especially in front of the cathedral and on Praça do Figueira). They have no meter—negotiate with the driver for a tour, or hire one for a point-to-point ride (they can be a little cheaper than a taxi and fit up to three). Tuk-tuks are most practical as a way to tailor your own private tour (€45/hour, €30 if demand is slow and the driver owns his own rig). The key is finding a likeable driver with good language skills and a little charm. The upside: They come with light guiding, can get you into little back lanes, let you hop on and off for quick visits and photo stops, and leave you where you like. The downside: You're contributing to something akin to an invasive weed that is blanketing the city with an annoying presence. Most are noisy and smelly, but you'll also see a few green, silent, electric "eco-tuk-tuks" that are more enticing (and more expensive).

Ways to Get from the Baixa Up to the Bairro Alto and Chiado

- Ride the Elevador da Glória funicular (a few blocks north of Rossio on Avenida da Liberdade, opposite the Hard Rock Café), or hike alongside the tracks if the funicular isn't running.
- Walk up lots of stairs from Rossio (due west of the central column).
- Taxi or Uber to the Miradouro de São Pedro de Alcântara.
- Take the escalators at the Baixa-Chiado Metro stop. You'll first ride down, then walk past the turnstiles for the Metro entrance, then ride back up, up, up.
- Catch trolley #28E from Rua da Conceição.
- Hike up Rua do Carmo from Rossio to Rua Garrett.
- Take the elevators inside the Armazéns mall (go through the low-profile doors at Rua do Crucifixo 89 or 113); ride to floor 5, and pop out at the bottom of Rua Garrett.
- Take the Elevador de Santa Justa, which goes right by the Convento do Carmo and the Chiado (can have long lines at busy times—but if it's jammed, other options are nearby).

BY BOAT

To get out on the Rio Tejo, take a sightseeing cruise or ride a public ferry. Either way, the main destination across the river is the port of Cacilhas (kah-SEE-lahsh). You can also hop a public ferry from Belém to Porto Brandão; see page 79.

Tourist Cruise: Yellow Boat—part of the big Yellow Bus tour company—offers a 1.5-hour loop that links Terreiro do Paço (near Praça do Comércio), Cacilhas, and Belém. You can hop on and off, but there are just five boats per day (€19/24 hours, discounts and combo-tickets with their bus tours and other offerings, mid-March-Oct only, details at www.yellowbustours.com).

Public Ferry Ride to Cacilhas: For a quick, cheap trip across the river with great city and bridge views in the company of Lisbon commuters rather than tourists, hop the ferry to Cacilhas from the Cais do Sodré station (a 10-minute walk from Praça do Comércio). At the terminal, follow signs to *Cacilhas*, not *Montijo* (€1.20 each way, 4/hour weekdays, fewer on weekends, signs say *partida*—departure—and *destino*). Either hop out for a look at the rough little industrial port, or stay on the boat for a 25-minute round-trip.

ON FOOT

Two walking-tour companies—Lisbon Walker and Inside Lisbon—offer excellent, affordable tours led by young, top-notch guides with a passion for sharing insights about their hometown.

Both have an easygoing style and small groups (generally 2-12 people); with either, you'll likely feel you've made a friend in your guide. These tours are time and money very well spent (both give my readers a discount).

Lisbon Walker

Standard tours include "Lisbon Revelation" (best 3-hour overview, with good coverage of Baixa and main squares, quick look at Bairro Alto, and trolley ride across town to Portas do Sol viewpoint); "Old Town" (2.5-hour walk through Alfama that examines the origins of Lisbon); and "Downtown" (2-3 hours, covers 1755 earthquake and rebirth of Lisbon). Each tour includes a shot of *ginjinha* or a tasty *pastel de nata*—two edible icons of Lisbon (€20/person, €15 with this book; tours run daily year-round—check schedule online; meet at northwest corner of Praça do Comércio near Rua do Arsenal, in front of the TI—see map on page 7, tel. 218-861-840, www.lisbonwalker.com).

Inside Lisbon

Tours include the "Best of Lisbon Walk" (good 3-hour highlights tour of the main squares, Chiado, and Alfama; €18/person, €13 with this book; daily year-round at 10:00) and food and wine tours (see "Food Tours," below). Most tours meet at the statue of Dom Pedro IV in the center of Rossio and last three to four hours (reserve a day ahead via website or phone, mobile 968-412-612, www.insidelisbon.com). They also offer daily private tours and day trips by minivan (€65/person, €60 with this book) to Sintra/Cascais (8 hours) and Obidos/Fátima (9 hours). You can organize a private city tour with them, or use their helpful website as a resource for seeing Lisbon on your own.

Lisbon Chill-Out Free Walking Tours

If you're looking for a free tour, choose from this young and creative group of local guides (skip Sandeman's, the big expat-led free tour company in town). Your Chill-Out guide is a local who will share cultural insights as you walk through the Bairro Alto, across the Baixa, and into the Alfama. It's refreshing to get a hometown perspective, and they are upfront about "it's not really free—you tip what you like at the end." Three-hour walks start in the Bairro Alto at the statue on Praça de Camões (look for the guide wearing the yellow travel bag) daily at 10:00 and 15:00 (www.lisbonfreetour.blogspot.pt).

FOOD TOURS

Guided food tours are trendy these days. Several companies offer three- to four-hour multistop tours that introduce you to lots of local food culture while filling your stomach at the same time. This is a quickly evolving scene, so it pays to do a little homework on the latest offerings. But I've enjoyed tours by several good outfits, listed below. In each case, the groups are small, the teaching is good, and—when you figure in the cost of the meal—the tours are a solid value.

Inside Lisbon offers three food-related itineraries: Their "Food and Wine Walk" makes five to six short, tasty, and memorable stand-up stops (€40/person, €35 with this book, 3 hours, Mon-Sat at 16:30). The "Sunset, Fado, and Tapas" walk includes an evening stroll and samples of local food and music (€65/person, €60 with this book, 4 hours, departs at 19:00, 5/week in summer, 2/week in winter). And their "Lisbon Experience Walk" is a tour through the Mouraria neighborhood with some food stops mixed in, ending with a ferry to Cacilhas for seafood (€45/person, €40 with this book, 4 hours, Mon-Sat at 10:30; www.insidelisbon.com).

Culinary Backstreets is slower-paced but more top-end, taking its time to delve into Lisbon's food scene and its culture. "Culinary Backstreets Essentials" focuses on the Mercado do Ribeira and nearby eateries and shops, ending in the Chiado. Because this company offers food tours throughout the world, it sets its prices in dollars ($95-110/person, 3.5 hours); their longer "Lisbon Awakens" tour passes through more neighborhoods ($130/person, 5.5 hours; www.culinarybackstreets.com).

Eat Drink Walk does a €70 tapas walk (5-6 stops in the Baixa), as well as a €85 "gourmet" walk (finer places in the Chiado; www.eatdrinkwalk.pt).

LOCAL GUIDES

Hiring a private local guide in Lisbon can be a wonderful luxury: Your guide will meet you at your hotel and tailor a tour to your interests. Especially with a small group, this can be a fine value. Guides charge roughly the same rates (€125/half-day, €200/day; car and driver options available). Delightful **Alex Almeida** runs **Your Friend in Lisbon** (group of 4 guides, mobile 919-292-151, www. yourfriendinlisbon.com, alex@yourfriendinlisbon.com). **Cristina Duarte** leads tours for my company and knows Lisbon well (mobile 919-316-242, www.lisbonbeyond.pt, acrismduarte@gmail. com). **Claudia da Costa,** who appears on my Lisbon TV show, is also excellent (mobile 965-560-216, claudiadacosta@hotmail.com). **Cristina Quental** is another fine local guide (mobile 919-922-480, anacristinaquental@hotmail.com).

Lisbon at a Glance

In Lisbon

▲▲▲**Alfama Stroll and the Castle** Tangled medieval streets topped by São Jorge Castle. See page 24.

▲▲▲**Baixa Stroll** The lower town—Lisbon's historic downtown—gridded with streets and dotted with major squares. See page 33.

▲▲▲**Bairro Alto and Chiado Stroll** The high town's views, churches, and Chiado fashion district. See page 43.

▲▲**Gulbenkian Museum** Lisbon's best museum, featuring an art collection spanning 5,000 years, from ancient Egypt to Impressionism to Art Nouveau. **Hours:** Wed-Mon 10:00-18:00, closed Tue. See page 56.

▲▲**Museum of Ancient Art** Portuguese paintings from the 15th- and 16th-century glory days. **Hours:** Tue-Sun 10:00-18:00, closed Mon. See page 60.

▲▲**Parque das Nações** Inviting waterfront park with a long promenade, modern mall, aquarium, and the Expo '98 fairgrounds. **Hours:** Park always open. See page 80.

▲**Fado Museum** The story of Portuguese folk music. **Hours:** Tue-Sun 10:00-18:00, closed Mon. See page 32.

▲**São Roque Church and Museum** Fine 16th-century Jesuit church with false dome ceiling, chapel made of precious stones, and a less-interesting museum. **Hours:** Mon 14:00-18:00, Tue-Sun 9:00-19:00—until 18:00 in winter, Thu until 20:00. See page 45.

▲**Lisbon Cathedral** From the outside, an impressive Romanesque fortress of God; inside, not much. **Hours:** Tue-Sat 9:00-19:00, Sun-Mon until 17:00. See page 53.

National Tile Museum Tons of artistic tiles, including a panorama of preearthquake Lisbon. **Hours:** Tue-Sun 10:00-18:00, closed Mon. See page 82.

Solar do Vinho do Porto Plush place selling tastes of the world's greatest selection of ports. **Hours:** Mon-Fri 11:00-24:00, Sat 14:00-24:00, closed Sun. See page 119.

São Jorge Castle Originally an eighth-century bastion, first built by the Moors, with kingly views at the highest point in town. **Hours:** Daily March-Oct 9:00-21:00, Nov-Feb until 18:00. See page 27.

Museum and School of Portuguese Decorative Arts Aristocratic household richly decorated in 15th- to 18th-century styles. **Hours:** Wed-Mon 10:00-17:00, closed Tue. See page 30.

Elevador de Santa Justa 150-foot-tall iron elevator offering a glittering city vista. **Hours:** Daily 7:00-23:00, until 22:00 in winter. See page 48.

In Belém
Note that all of these sights—except the Monument to the Discoveries—are closed on Monday year-round.

▲▲▲**Monastery of Jerónimos** King Manuel's giant 16th-century, white limestone church and monastery, with remarkable cloister and the explorer Vasco da Gama's tomb. **Hours:** Tue-Sun 10:00-18:30, Oct-April until 17:30, closed Mon. See page 68.

▲▲**National Coach Museum** Dozens of carriages, from simple to opulent, displaying the evolution of coaches from 1600 on. **Hours:** Tue-Sun 10:00-18:00, closed Mon. See page 65.

▲**Maritime Museum** Salty selection of exhibits on the ships and navigational tools of the Age of Discovery. **Hours:** Daily 10:00-18:00, Oct-April until 17:00. See page 74.

▲**Monument to the Discoveries** Giant riverside monument honoring the explorers who brought Portugal great power and riches centuries ago. **Hours:** May-Sept daily 10:00-19:00; Oct-April Tue-Sun 10:00-18:00, closed Mon. See page 75.

▲**Belém Tower** Consummate Manueline building with a worthwhile view up 120 steps. **Hours:** May-Sept Tue-Sun 10:00-18:30, off-season until 17:30, closed Mon. See page 78.

Neighborhood Walks in Lisbon

The essential Lisbon is easily and enjoyably covered in three ▲▲▲ self-guided walking tours through three downtown neighborhoods: Alfama, Baixa, and Bairro Alto/Chiado. You can do them as individual walks, or lace them together into a single tour (allow a minimum of five hours for all three, but could be done as a more leisurely all-day experience—or, for maximum lingering, spread it over two days). You can do the walks in any order, but starting with the Alfama lets you get to the castle before the crowds hit (and avoid ticket lines), kicking things off with a grand city view from Lisbon's fortified birthplace. And you'll finish in the liveliest quarter for evening fun—the Bairro Alto/Chiado.

∩ You can download a free Rick Steves audio tour that covers some of the same territory as these walks, from Praça do Comércio through the Baixa, and up through the highlights of the Bairro Alto.

ALFAMA STROLL AND THE CASTLE

On this ▲▲▲ walk, you'll explore the Alfama, the colorful sailors' quarter that dates back to the age of Visigoth occupation, from the sixth to eighth centuries A.D. This was a bustling district during the Moorish period, and eventually became the home of Lisbon's fishermen and mariners (and of the poet Luís de Camões, who wrote, "Our lips meet easily, high across the narrow street"). The Alfama's tangled street plan, one of the few features of Lisbon to survive the 1755 earthquake, helps make the neighborhood a cobbled playground of Old World color. The best times to visit are during the busy midmorning market, or in the cooler late afternoon or early evening, when the streets teem with residents. While much of the Alfama's grittiness has been cleaned up in recent years, it remains one of Europe's more photogenic neighborhoods.

Getting There: This walk begins at the highest point in town, São Jorge Castle. Get to the castle gate by **taxi** (€6); by **minibus #737** from Praça da Figueira; or by two free **elevator rides** up from the Baixa and then a short uphill walk. To find the elevators, head to Rua dos Fanqueiros and go through the easy-to-miss door at #178 (for location, see map on page 26; you'll see faint, white lettering spelling out *elevador castelo* on the red rooftop—illuminated at night). Ride the elevator to the top floor and exit, angling left across the street and through the little square. Then head up Largo Chão do Loureiro, where you'll see the second elevator (*elevador castelo;* handy supermarket with WC at bottom, view café and fine panoramic terrace at top). When exiting the second elevator, simply follow brown *Castelo de S. Jorge* signs up to the castle (right, then hooking left; about 8 minutes uphill).

LISBON

Alternatively, **trolleys** #28E and #12E go to Largo Santa Luzia and Largo das Portas do Sol, respectively, a few blocks below the walk's starting point—it's a fun trip, but still a steep hike up to the castle.

❶ São Jorge Castle Gate and Fortified Castle Town

The formidable gate to the castle is part of a fortification that, these days, surrounds three things: the view terrace, the small town that stood within the walls, and the castle itself. The ticket office and the turnstile are situated so that those without a ticket are kept away from the view terrace and castle proper (castle entry-€8.50, daily March-Oct 9:00-21:00, Nov-Feb until 18:00).

If money is tight, the castle and view are skippable—the castle is just stark, rebuilt ruins from the Salazar era, and while the hill-capping park has a commanding view, there are other fine views coming up...just jump ahead to stop #4 on this walk.

• *If you decide to go in, follow the cobbles uphill past the first lanes of old Lisbon to the yellow ticket office, and then into the...*

❷ Miradouro de São Jorge (Viewpoint)

Enjoy the grand view. The Rio Tejo is one of five main rivers in Portugal, four of which come from Spain. (Only the Mondego

River, which passes through Coimbra, originates inside Portuguese territory, in the Serra de Estrela.) While Portugal and Spain generally have very good relations, a major sore point is the control of all this water. From here, you have a good view of the Golden Gate-like 25th of April Bridge, which leads south to the Cristo Rei statue (described on page 84). Past the bridge, on a clear day, you can barely see the Monument to the Discoveries and the Belém Tower (under and past the bridge on north side).

Look up at the statue marking the center of this terrace. **Afonso Henriques,** a warlord with a strong personal army, was the founder of Portugal. In 1147, he besieged this former Moorish castle until the hungry, thirsty residents gave in. Every Portuguese school-kid knows the story of this man—a Reconquista hero and their country's first king.

Stroll inland along the **ramparts** for a more extensive view of Pombal's Lisbon, described in a circa 1963, tiled panorama-chart (which lacks the big 25th of April Bridge—it was built in 1969). From Praça do Comércio on the water, the grid streets of the Baixa lead up to the tree-lined Avenida da Liberdade and the big Edward

LISBON

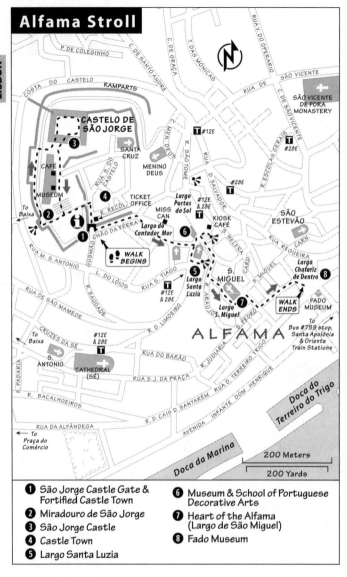

Alfama Stroll

❶ São Jorge Castle Gate & Fortified Castle Town
❷ Miradouro de São Jorge
❸ São Jorge Castle
❹ Castle Town
❺ Largo Santa Luzia
❻ Museum & School of Portuguese Decorative Arts
❼ Heart of the Alfama (Largo de São Miguel)
❽ Fado Museum

VII Park, on the far right. Locate city landmarks, such as the Elevador de Santa Justa (the Eiffel-style elevator in front of the ruined Convento do Carmo) and the sloping white roof of Rossio station.
• *Continue walking along the viewpoint, passing several old cannons. Just after going under the second arch (just before the café terrace), take a right into the mostly ruined courtyard of...*

❸ São Jorge Castle

While the first settlements here go back to the 7th century B.C., this castle dates to the 11th century when Moors built it to house

their army and provide a safe haven for their elites in times of siege. After Afonso Henriques took the castle in 1147, Portugal's royalty lived here for several centuries. The sloping walls—typical of castles from this period—were designed to withstand 14th-century cannonballs. In the 16th century, the kings moved to their palace on Praça do Comércio, and the castle became a military garrison. Despite suffering major damage in the 1755 earthquake, the castle later served another stint as a military garrison. In the 20th century, it became a national monument.

The strolling **peacocks** remind visitors that exotic birds like these came to Lisbon originally as trophies of the great 16th-century voyages and discoveries. (Today the jaded birds ignore the tourists and cry as if to remember some long-forgotten castle captives.)

Bear left to find the **inner castle**—the largely intact, boxy, crenelated fort in the middle. There's little to see inside the empty shell, but it's fun to climb up the steep stone steps to scramble around the top of the ramparts and towers, with ever-changing views of Lisbon, the Alfama, and the castle itself. (Up top, you'll also find a thrillingly low-tech camera obscura, which is demonstrated twice hourly—times and languages posted.)

As you explore the castle's inner sanctum, imagine it lined with simple wooden huts. The imposing part of the castle is the exterior. The builders' strategy was to focus on making the castle appear so formidable that its very existence was enough to discourage any attack. If you know where to look, you can still see stones laid by ancient Romans, Visigoths, and Moors. The Portuguese made the most substantial contribution, with a wall reaching all the way to the river to withstand anticipated Spanish attacks.

When finished, head back out the inner castle gate, and continue straight ahead toward the castle's entrance. On your right, you'll pass the café, then the humble **museum.** This houses archaeological finds from the 7th century B.C. to the 18th century, with emphasis on the Moorish period in the 11th and 12th centuries. You'll also see 18th-century tiles from an age when Portugal was flush with money from the gold, diamonds, and sugarcane of its colony Brazil. While simple, the museum has nice displays and descriptions.

• *Leave the castle. Across the ramp from the castle entrance is a tidy little castle district, worth a wander for its peaceful lanes and a chance to enjoy the Manueline architecture.*

❹ Castle Town

Just outside the castle turnstile is the tiny neighborhood within the castle walls built to give Moorish elites refuge from sieges and, later, for Portuguese nobles to live close to their king. While it's partly taken over by cute shops and cafés, if you wander up Rua de Santa Cruz do Castelo (to the left as you exit the castle) and stroll into its back lanes, you can enjoy a peaceful bit of Portugal's past. (Make a big clockwise loop back to where you entered—you can't get lost, as it's within the walls and there's only one way in or out.) Most of the houses date from the Middle Ages. Poking around, go on a cultural scavenger hunt. Look for: 1) clever, space-efficient, triangular contraptions for drying clothes (hint: see the glass bottle bottoms in the wall used to prop the sticks out when in use); 2) Benfica soccer team flag (that's the team favored by Lisbon's working class—an indication that the upper class no longer chooses to live here); 3) short doors that were tall enough for people back when these houses were built; and 4) noble family crests over doors—dating to when important families wanted to be close to the king.

When you're ready to leave, make your way back to where you started, and head down the ramp to return to the real world. On your way out, just before exiting the lower gate, notice the little statue in the niche on your right. This is the castle's namesake: **St. George** (São Jorge; pronounced "sow ZHOR-zh") hailed from Turkey and was known for fighting valiantly (he's often portrayed slaying a dragon). When the Christian noble Afonso Henriques called for help to eliminate the Moors from his newly founded country of Portugal, the Crusaders who helped him prayed to St. George...and won.

• *Exiting the castle complex grounds, bear left and walk along the wall, then turn right down the second street, Travessa do Chão da Feira. Follow this striped lane downhill through **Largo do Contador Mor**. This small, car-clogged square has a Parisian ambience, some touristy outdoor restaurants serving grilled sardines, and the inviting little **Miss Can** shop and eatery—where traditional Portuguese canned fish gets a modern twist (for ideas on lunching here, see page 115).*

Exit the square at the bottom, continue downhill 50 yards farther, pass the trolley tracks, and jog right around the little church to reach a superb Alfama viewpoint at...

❺ Largo Santa Luzia

From this square (with a stop for trolleys #12E and #28E), admire the panoramic view from the small terrace, **Miradouro de Santa**

Pombal's Lisbon

In 1750, lazy King José I (r. 1750-1777) turned the government over to a minor noble, the Marquês de Pombal (1699-1782). Talented, ambitious, and handsome, Pombal was praised as a reformer, but reviled for his ruthless tactics. Having learned modern ways as the ambassador to Britain, he battled Church repression and promoted the democratic ideals of the Enlightenment, but enforced his policies with arrests, torture, and executions. He expelled the Jesuits to keep them from monopolizing the education system, put the bishop of Coimbra in prison, and broke off relations with the pope. When the earthquake of 1755 leveled the city, within a month Pombal had kicked off major rebuilding in much of today's historic downtown—featuring a grid plan for the world's first quake-proof buildings. In 1777, the king died, and the controversial Pombal was dismissed.

Luzia, where old-timers play cards and Romeos strum their guitars amid lots of tiles.

In the distance to the left, the **Vasco da Gama Bridge** (opened in 1998, described on page 82) connects Lisbon with new, modern bedroom communities south of the river.

At your feet sprawls the **Alfama** neighborhood. We'll head that way soon, to explore its twisty lanes. Where the Alfama hits the river, notice the recently built embankment. It reclaimed 100 yards of land from the river to make a modern port, used these days to accommodate Lisbon's growing cruise ship industry.

On the wall of the church behind you, notice two 18th-century **tiles.** The one on the left shows the preearthquake Praça do Comércio, with the royal palace (on the left)—it was completely destroyed in the 1755 quake. The other tile (ten steps away, to the right) depicts the reconquest of Lisbon from the Moors by Afonso Henriques. You can see the Portuguese hero, Martim Moniz, who let himself be crushed in the castle door to hold it open for his comrades. Notice the panicky Moors inside realizing that their castle is about to be breeched by invading Crusaders. It was a bad day for the Moors. (A stairway here leads up to a tiny view terrace with a café.)

For an even better city view, hike back around the church and walk out to the seaside end of the **Miradouro das Portas do Sol** catwalk. The huge, frilly building dominating the ridge on the far left is the Monastery of São Vicente, constructed around 1600 by the Spanish king Philip II, who left his mark here with this tribute to St. Vincent. A few steps away, next to a statue of St. Vincent, is a kiosk café where you can enjoy perhaps the most scenic cup of coffee in town.

• *Across the street from the café, you'll find the...*

❻ Museum and School of Portuguese Decorative Arts

The Museum and School of Portuguese Decorative Arts (Museu Escola de Artes Decorativas Portuguesas) offers a stroll through

a richly decorated, aristocratic household. The palace, filled with 15th- to 18th-century fine art, offers the best chance for visitors to experience what a noble home looked like during Lisbon's glory days. Inside, a coach on the ground level is "Berlin style," with a state-of-the-art suspension system, on leather straps. The grand stairway leads upstairs past 18th-century glazed tiles (Chinese-style blue-and-white was in vogue) into a world of colonial riches. Portuguese aristocrats had a special taste for "Indo-Portuguese" decorative arts: objects of exotic woods such as teak or rosewood, and inlaid with shell or ivory, made along the sea routes of the age (€4, Wed-Mon 10:00-17:00, closed Tue, Largo das Portas do Sol 2, tel. 218-814-640, www.fress.pt).

From here, it's downhill all the way. From Largo das Portas do Sol (the plaza with the statue of local patron St. Vincent, near the

kiosk café on the terrace), go down the loooong **stairs** (Rua Norberto de Araújo, between the church and the catwalk). A few steps down on the left, under the big arch, notice the public WCs and the fun, vivid **cartoon mural** illustrating Lisbon's history (if you know the key dates, you can enjoy it even without understanding Portuguese).

The massive eighth-century **fortified wall** (on the right of the staircase) once marked the boundary of Moorish Lisbon. Consider that the great stones on your right were stacked here over a thousand years ago. At the bottom of the wall, continue downhill, then turn left at the railing...and go down more stairs.

• *Explore downhill from here. The main thoroughfare, a concrete stepped lane called Escadinhas de São Miguel, funnels you to the Alfama's main square.*

❼ The Heart of the Alfama

This square, **Largo de São Miguel,** is the best place to observe a slice of Alfama life. When city leaders rebuilt the rest of Lisbon

after the 1755 quake, this neighborhood was left out and consequently retains its tangled medieval streets.

If you've got the time, **explore the Alfama** from this central square. Its urban-jungle roads are squeezed into confusing alleys—the labyrinthine street plan was designed to frustrate invaders (and guidebook researchers trying to get up to the castle). What was defensive then is atmospheric now. Bent houses comfort each other in their romantic shabbiness, and the air drips with laundry and the smell of clams. Get lost. Poke aimlessly, peek through windows, buy a fish. Locals hang plastic water bags from windows in the summer to try to keep away the flies. Favorite saints decorate doors to protect families. St. Peter, protector of fishermen, is big in the Alfama. Churches are generally closed, since they share a priest. As children have very little usable land for a good soccer game, goalposts are painted onto the stairs.

The tiny balconies were limited to "one-and-a-half hands" in width. A strictly enforced health initiative was designed to keep

the town open and well-ventilated. If you see carpets hanging out to dry, it means a laundry is nearby. Because few homes have their own, every neighborhood has a public laundry and bathroom. Until recently, in the early morning hours, the streets were busy with residents in pajamas, heading for these public baths. Today, many are choosing to live elsewhere, lured by modern conveniences unavailable here, and the old flats became congested with immigrant laborers who came during the construction boom a decade ago. Today, with the bad economy, they are moving on in search of employment. In just a couple of generations, the demographics have changed—from fishermen's families to immigrants to young bohemians.

Traditionally the neighborhood here was tightly knit, with

families routinely sitting down to communal dinners in the streets. Feuds, friendships, and gossip were all intense. Historically, when a woman's husband died, she wore black for the rest of her life—a tradition that's just about gone.

The Alfama hosts Lisbon's most popular outdoor party on St. Anthony's Day (June 13). Imagine tables set up everywhere, bands playing, bright plastic flowers strung across the squares, and all the grilled sardines *(sardinhas grelhadas)* you can eat. The rustic paintings of festive characters (with hints of Moorish style) remind locals of past parties, and strings and wires overhead await future festival dates when the neighborhood will again be festooned with colorful streamers.

While there are plenty of traditional festivals here, the most action on the Alfama calendar is the insane, annual mountain-bike street race from the castle to the sea (which you can see hurtle by in two minutes on YouTube; search "Lisboa downtown race").

Continue exploring downhill from here. Just below the square you'll see the recommended amateur fado restaurant (A Baiuca). Then, a few steps further downhill, you'll hit the cobbled pedestrian lane, **Rua São Pedro.** This darkest of the Alfama's streets, in nearly perpetual shade, was the logical choice for the neighborhood's fish market. Modern hygiene requirements (which forbid outdoor stalls) killed the market, but it's still a characteristic lane to explore.

• *Turn left and follow Rua São Pedro out of the Alfama to the square called Largo do Chafariz de Dentro and, across the street, the...*

❽ Fado Museum

This museum, rated ▲, tells the story of fado in English—with a great chance to hear these wailing fisherwomen's blues. Three levels of wall murals show three generations of local fado stars, and the audioguide lets you listen to the Billie Holidays of Portugal (€5, includes audioguide, Tue-Sun 10:00-18:00, closed Mon, Largo do Chafariz de Dentro, tel. 218-823-470, www.museudofado.pt).

• *This walk is over. To get back downtown (or to Praça do Comércio, where the next walk starts), walk a block to the main waterfront drag and cruise-ship harbor (facing the museum, go left around it) where busy Avenida Infante Dom Henrique leads back to Praça do Comércio (to the right). While it's a 15-minute walk or quick taxi ride to Praça do Comércio, just to the left is a bus stop; hop on any bus for two stops, and you're there in moments. (Also, bus #759 goes on to Praça dos Restauradores.)*

BAIXA STROLL

This ▲▲▲ walk covers the highlights of Lisbon's historic down-town, the Baixa, which fills a flat valley between two hills. The

district slopes gently from the wa-terfront up to the Rossio, Praça dos Restauradores, Avenida da Liber-dade, and the newer town. The walk starts at Praça do Comércio and ends at Praça dos Restauradores.

• *Start your walk at the statue of King José I in the center of Praça do Comércio. Find a spot of shade in José's shadow (or take cover under the arcades) and read a bit about the Baixa's history.*

Background: After the disastrous 1755 earthquake, the Baixa district was rebuilt on a grid street plan. The uniform and utilitar-ian Pombaline architecture (named after the Marquês de Pombal, the chief minister who rebuilt the city—see sidebar, earlier) feels almost military. That's because it is. The Baixa was constructed by military engineers who had experience building garrison towns overseas. The new Lisbon featured the architecture of conquest—simple to assemble, economical, with all the pieces easy to ship. The 18th-century buildings you'd see in Mozambique and Brazil are interchangeable with those in Lisbon.

The buildings are all uniform, with the same number of floors and standard facades. They were designed to survive the next earthquake, with stone firewalls and wooden frameworks that had flexible crisscross beams. The priorities were to rebuild fast, cheap, and shake-proof.

If it had been left up to the people, who believed the earth-quake was a punishment from God, they would have rebuilt their churches bigger and more impressive than ever. But Pombal was a practical military man with a budget, a timeline, and an awareness of his society's limits. He didn't want church-building to compro-mise the needs of the people. In those austere postearthquake days, Pombal got his way.

The Baixa has three squares—two preearthquake (Comér-cio and Rossio) and one added later (Figueira)—and three main streets: Prata (silver), Aurea (gold), and Augusta (relating the Por-tuguese king to a Roman emperor). The former maze of the Jewish quarter was eliminated, but the area has many streets named for the crafts and shops once found there.

The Baixa's pedestrian streets, inviting cafés, bustling shops, and elegant old storefronts give the district a certain charm. City-government subsidies make sure the old businesses stay around, but modern ones find a way to creep in. I find myself doing laps up

LISBON

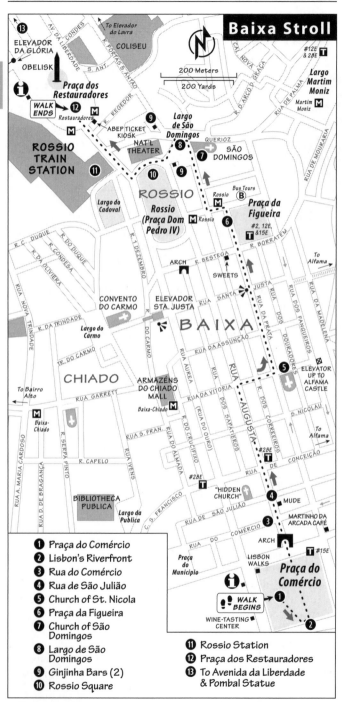

Baixa Stroll

ELEVADOR DA GLÓRIA

OBELISK

Praça dos Restauradores

WALK ENDS

ROSSIO TRAIN STATION

To Elevador do Lavra

COLISEU

200 Meters
200 Yards

Largo Martim Moniz

Martim Moniz

ABEP TICKET KIOSK

NAT'L THEATER

Largo de São Domingos

SÃO DOMINGOS

QUERIOZ

Bus Tours

Praça da Figueira

Rossio

Largo do Cadoval

ROSSIO

Rossio (Praça Dom Pedro IV)

BAIXA

CONVENTO DO CARMO

ELEVADOR STA. JUSTA

ARCH

SWEETS

RUA SANTA JUSTA

Largo do Carmo

CHIADO

ARMAZÉNS DO CHIADO MALL

Baixa-Chiado

Baixa-Chiado

ELEVADOR UP TO ALFAMA CASTLE

To Bairro Alto

RUA GARRETT

To Alfama

"HIDDEN CHURCH"

MUDE

BIBLIOTHECA PUBLICA

Largo da Publica

MARTINHO DA ARCADA CAFÉ

ARCH

LISBON WALKS

Praça do Município

Praça do Comércio

WALK BEGINS

WINE-TASTING CENTER

1. Praça do Comércio
2. Lisbon's Riverfront
3. Rua do Comércio
4. Rua de São Julião
5. Church of St. Nicola
6. Praça da Figueira
7. Church of São Domingos
8. Largo de São Domingos
9. Ginjinha Bars (2)
10. Rossio Square
11. Rossio Station
12. Praça dos Restauradores
13. To Avenida da Liberdade & Pombal Statue

and down Rua Augusta in a people-watching stupor. Its delightful ambience is perfect for strolling.

• *Now turn your attention to the square itself.*

❶ Praça do Comércio (Commerce Square)

At this riverfront square bordering the Baixa—along the gateway to Lisbon—ships used to dock and sell their goods. This was the

site of Portugal's royal palace for 200 preearthquake years, but after the 1755 earthquake/tsunami/fire, the jittery king fled to more stable Belém, never to return. These days, government ministries ring Praça do Comércio. It's also the departure point for city bus and tram tours, and boats that cruise along the Rio Tejo. The area opposite the harbor was conceived as a residential neighborhood for the upper class, but they chose the suburbs. Today, the square has two names ("Palace Square" and "Commerce Square") and little real life. Locals consider it just a big place to pass through.

The statue is **José I,** the king who gave control of the government to his chief minister, the Marquês de Pombal. Built 20 years after the quake, it shows the king on his horse, with Pombal (on the medallion), looking at their port. The horse (symbolic of triumph) stomps on snakes (symbolic of evil—perhaps Protestants... or troublemaking noble families), while the elephant represents the Portuguese empire's colonies in India and Africa. In its glory days, this city was where east met west.

The big arch marking the inland side of the square is Lisbon's **Arch of Triumph** (with Vasco da Gama on the left and Pombal on the right). Disregarding his usual austerity, Pombal restored some of the city's Parisian-style grandeur at this central approach into downtown.

Facing the Arch of Triumph, get oriented to a few landmarks on the square (moving from left to right):

At 9 o'clock is the **Wines of Portugal Tasting Room,** a nonprofit wine-appreciation venue. Sixteen local wines are offered with English descriptions above each tap, with a helpful attendant happy to explain things. To taste, you buy a chip card (€3 minimum), take a glass, and serve yourself samples of eight whites, eight reds, a green *(vinho verde),* and a port (each €0.50 and up; Mon-Thu 11:00-19:00, Fri-Sat until 20:00, closed Sun).

At 10 o'clock is the **TI.**

At 2 o'clock, under the arcade just right of the arch, is **Martinho da Arcada,** a fine option for a coffee, pastry, or snack. It was founded in 1782—when the wealthy would come here to savor early ice cream made with mountain snow, lemon, and spices. While it has a fancy restaurant, I'd enjoy just a coffee and pastry in its café bar. This place was one of poet Fernando Pessoa's old haunts (they display a few Pessoa artifacts, lots of old photos, and a shrine-like table that was his favorite). In the early 20th century, painters, writers, and dreamers shared revolutionary ideas here over coffee (Praça do Comércio 8, at the corner of Rua da Prata).

At 3 o'clock is the much-promoted **"Lisbon Story Center,"** a childish exhibit with no artifacts—you pay €8 to stand for an hour looking at animated history on computer screens. Nearby is another branch of the **TI** (in case the first one is too crowded).

And at 5 o'clock is the **Terreiro do Paço Metro stop** (see the red *M* on a post).

• *Before moving on, use the crosswalk at the bottom of the big square for a quick look at...*

❷ Lisbon's Riverfront

An inviting balustrade and a pair of Pombaline pillars—symbolizing Lisbon's gateway to the sea—mark a little pier (called the Cais das Colunas) that offers a fine, water-level view of the Tejo riverscape. To your left is the busy Terreiro do Paço ferry terminal—one of many that connect commuters to the far side of the river. To your right are the 25th of April Bridge and Cristo Rei statue. Down here at water level, you can really see that the Tejo is a tidal river—the Atlantic is just around the bend (past the bridge). At low tide, the humble little rocky beach reveals worlds of sea life in rocky pools. Any tide poolers out today?

• *Now, head back up through the square, cross the busy street, pass under the big arch, and walk down Rua Augusta into the Baixa district. (Skip the chance to pay to go to the top of the arch—it affords only a mediocre view from its empty rooftop.)*

The first cross-street you meet is...

❸ Rua do Comércio

Look right to see the old **cathedral** with its Romanesque fortress-like crenellations (described on page 53). Notice that many of the surrounding buildings are in the austere architectural style adopted immediately after the earthquake. Exterior decoration was adopted here in Lisbon only in the 19th century, after the Portuguese in colonial Brazil found that the tiles protected against humidity.

The characteristic black-and-white cobbled **sidewalk** *(calçada)* is uniquely Portuguese. These mosaic limestone and basalt cobbles were first cut and laid by 19th-century prison laborers. To this day patterns are chosen from a book of acceptable designs. As the stones are slippery and expensive to maintain, the city government is talking about replacing them with modern pavement. And locals are crying out to keep the tradition.

Across the street, on the right, you'll pass the **MUDE,** Lisbon's museum of design (free, Tue-Sun 10:00-18:00, closed Mon). Filling the Art Deco ground floor of a former bank, it offers a quick, well-described-in-English, one-floor stroll through 20th-century fashion. Special exhibits are on other floors, and a huge bank vault in the basement is often part of the show.

• *The next cross-street is...*

❹ Rua de São Julião

Churches are scarce in the postearthquake Baixa. There's one about 30 yards to the left down Rua de São Julião (on right side

of street—it's hiding; look for the triangular pediment over the door). Only a few of the quake-destroyed churches were rebuilt, and those were incorporated into the prevailing no-nonsense facades to better match the rest of the street. You'll notice that the Baixa district is struggling to stay vital, with the upper floors of many buildings now mostly empty. Look up for evidence of how downtown Lisbon's population is shrinking, as more people move to the suburbs.

At the next block, **Rua da Conceição,** there's a stop for the handy trolley #28E. Ahead on the right (in the windows of the Millennium Bank) are Roman artifacts—a reminder that Lisbon's history goes way back.

• *Go two more blocks to the intersection with Rua da Vitoria. Turn right and walk two blocks to Rua da Prata, where you'll see the camouflaged...*

❺ Church of St. Nicola (Igreja de São Nicolau)

Notice how a typical church facade was allowed to face the square, but on the street-front side, the entire exterior is disguised with green tiles, as just another stretch of post-earthquake Baixa architecture. Several of the fine, tiled buildings on this square have

The Lisbon Earthquake of 1755

At 9:40 in the morning on Sunday, November 1—All Saints'
Day—an underwater earthquake
estimated to be close to 9.0 in mag-
nitude occurred off the southern
Portuguese coast. Massive tremors
rumbled through Lisbon, punctuat-
ed by three main jolts. The quake
came midway through Mass, when
devout locals filled the churches.
Ten minutes later, thousands lay
dead under the rubble.

Along the waterfront, shaken
survivors scrambled aboard boats to sail to safety. They were
met by a 20-foot wall of water, the first wave of a tsunami that
rushed up the Rio Tejo. The ravaging water capsized ships,
swept people off the docks, crested over the seawall, and
crashed 800 feet inland.

The violent tremors were felt throughout Europe—as far
away as Finland. Imagine a disaster similar to 2004's Indian
Ocean earthquake and tsunami, devastating Portugal's capital
city.

After the quake, the city turned into an inferno, as over-
turned cooking fires and fallen church candles ignited raging
fires. The flames blazed for five days, ravaging the downtown
from the Bairro Alto across Rossio to the castle atop the Alfama.

Of Lisbon's 270,000 citizens, over 10,000 may have per-
ished, and two-thirds of the city was leveled. The city's biggest buildings—its churches, designed to connect earth with
heaven—had simply collapsed, crushing the faithful. Under-
standably, the quake shook conservative Portugal's moral and
spiritual underpinnings. Had God punished Lisbon for the Inquisition killings carried out on nearby Praça do Comércio? To
the people of the time, it must have felt like the Apocalypse.

King José I was so affected by the earthquake that he
moved his entire court to an elaborate complex of tents in the
foothills of Belém and resisted living indoors for the rest of his
life. He left his energetic (and eventually dictatorial) second-
in-command—his chief minister Marquês de Pombal—the task
of rebuilding. For more on Pombal, see "Pombal's Lisbon,"
earlier.

been refurbished. In fact, the one at the very top of the square hides
a free elevator that takes you partway up to the castle atop the Alfama.

• Head left down Rua da Prata toward the statue marking Praça da
Figueira. At Rua de Santa Justa, look left for a good view of Elevador
de Santa Justa before continuing straight to the square.

❻ Praça da Figueira (Fig Tree Square)

This was the site of a huge hospital destroyed in the earthquake. With no money to replace the hospital, the space was left open

until the late 1880s, when it was filled with a big iron-framed market (similar to Barcelona's La Boqueria). That structure was torn down decades ago, leaving the square you see today.

The big building on the left is run-down—after 50 years of rent control, many landowners are demoralized and do nothing to fix up their property. Buildings like this are often either vacant or occupied by old pensioners living out their lives amid increasingly decrepit conditions. By contrast, the right side (under the castle) is more lived-in and vibrant.

The nearby **Confeitaria Nacional** shop (on the corner of the square, 20 yards to your left) is a venerable palace of sweets little changed since the 19th century. In the window is a display of *"conventuel* sweets"—special nun-made treats often consisting of sugar and egg yolks (historically, the nuns, who used the egg whites to starch their laundry, had an abundance of yolks). Consider a light lunch here in the upstairs dining room (see page 108 for details).

The square is a transportation hub, with stops for minibus #737 to the castle; the old trolley #12E to the Alfama viewpoint (see page 16 for a self-guided trolley tour); the modern trolley #15E and bus #714 heading out to Belém; and the touristic hop-on, hop-off buses.

Walk to the far-left corner of the square, past skateboarders oblivious to its historical statue—Portugal's King João I on a horse. Continue straight out of the square on **Rua Dom Antão de Almada**. This lane has several characteristic shops. Pop into the classic cod shop (on the left at #1C—you'll smell it). Cod *(bacalhau)* is part of Portugal's heritage as a nation of seafaring explorers: Salted cod could keep for a year on a ship. Just soak in water to rinse out the salt and enjoy. The adjacent ham counter serves *pata negra (presunto ibérico)* from acorn-fed pigs—the very best. The *alheira* sausage, made with game instead of pork, was a favorite among Lisbon's Jews back when they needed to fake being Christians (during the forced conversions of the Inquisition era).

• *At the end of the lane stands a big church facing another square.*

❼ Church of São Domingos

A center of the Inquisition in the 1600s, this is now one of Lisbon's most active churches (daily 7:30-19:00). The evocative interior—

more or less rebuilt from the ruins left by the 1755 earthquake—reminds visitors of that horrible All Saints' Day Sunday, when most of the city was at Mass and the earth rolled. Across the city, heavy stone church walls like these collapsed on their congregants. Standing at the back of the nave, you can see which parts of the original stone walls remained standing. The black soot on the walls and the charred stonework at the altar recalls the horrible fires that followed the earthquake. Our Lady of Fátima is Portugal's most popular saint, and her chapel (in the left rear of the church) always has the most candles. Her statue is accompanied by two of the three children to whom she miraculously appeared (the third was still alive when this chapel was made and so is not shown in heaven with the saint).

• *Step into the square just beyond the church.*

❽ Largo de São Domingos

This area was just outside of the old town walls—long a place where people gathered to keep watering holes busy and enjoy bohemian entertainment. Today the square is home to classic old bars (like the *ginjinha* bar described next) and a busy "eating lane," Rua das Portas de Santo Antão (kitty-corner from where you entered the square, to the right of the National Theater on the far side of the square).

A stone monument on the square remembers the Jewish massacre of 1506. Many Jews expelled from Spain in 1492 took refuge in Portugal. But when a drought ravaged the country, Lisbonites killed several thousand of them on this square.

The city's 16th-century slave market also took place here, but the square is now a meeting point for the city's African community—immigrants from former Portuguese colonies such as Angola, Mozambique, and Portuguese Guinea. They hang out, trade news from home, and watch the tourists go by.

• *At the corner nearest the big adjoining square, find the colorful little hole-in-the-wall tavern serving a traditional berry brandy.*

❾ Liquid Sightseeing

Ginjinha (zheen-ZHEEN-yah) is a favorite Lisbon drink. While nuns baked sweets, the monks took care of quenching thirsts

with this sweet liquor, made from the *ginja* berry (like a sour cherry), sugar, cinnamon, and brandy. It's now sold for €1.40 a shot in funky old shops throughout downtown. Buy it with or without berries (*com elas* or *sem elas*—that's "with them" or "without them") and *gelada* (if you want it poured from a chilled bottle). In Portugal, when people are impressed by the taste of something, they say, *"Sabe que nem ginjas"*—literally "It tastes like *ginja*," but meaning "finger-lickin' good." The oldest *ginjinha* joint in town is a colorful hole-in-the-wall at Largo de São Domingos 8. If you hang around the bar long enough, you'll see them refill the bottle from an enormous vat. (Another *ginjinha* bar, Ginjinha sem Rival, serves the prized *eduardinho* liqueur, considered the most authentic; it's just across the square, at the start of the restaurant row—Rua das Portas de Santo Antão—at #7.)

• *The big square around the corner (fronting the National Theater) is called...*

❿ Rossio

Lisbon's historic center, Rossio, is still the city's bustling cultural heart. Given its elongated shape, historians believe it was a Roman racetrack 2,000 years ago; these days,

cars circle the loop instead of chariots. It's home to the colonnaded National Theater, American fast-food chains, and street vendors who can shine your shoes, laminate your documents, and sell you cheap watches, autumn chestnuts, and lottery tickets. The column in the square's center honors Pedro IV—king of Portugal and emperor of Brazil. (Many maps refer to the square as Praça Dom Pedro IV, but residents always just call it Rossio, for the train station at one corner.)

The square once held a palace that functioned as the headquarters of the Inquisition. It was demolished, and in an attempt to erase its memory, the National Theater was built in its place.

From here you can see the Elevador de Santa Justa and the ruined convent breaking the city skyline. Notice the fine stone patterns in the pavement—evoking waves encountered by the great explorers. (If you're prone to seasickness, don't look down as you cross the square.)

• *Crossing the square in front of the National Theater, you see Rossio station.*

⓫ Rossio Station

The circa-1900 facade of Rossio station is Neo-Manueline. You can read the words *"Estação Central"* (central station) carved on its striking horseshoe arches. Find the statue of King Sebastian in the center of two arches (he may be temporarily gone for restoration). This romantic, dashing, and young soldier-king was lost in 1580 in an ill-fated crusade to Africa. As Sebastian left no direct heir, the crown ended up with Philip II of Spain, who became Philip I of

Portugal. The Spanish king promised to give back the throne if Sebastian ever turned up—and ever since, the Portuguese have dreamed that Sebastian will return, restoring their national greatness. Even today, in a crisis, the Portuguese like to think that their Sebastian will save the day—he's the symbol of being ridiculously hopeful.

• *Just uphill from Rossio station is Praça dos Restauradores, at the bottom of Lisbon's long and grand Avenida da Liberdade. Between Rossio station and the square is Lisbon's oldest hotel, the **Avenida Palace.** Built as a terminus hotel at the same time as Rossio station, it has a fun interior, with an elegant yet inviting oasis of a bar/lounge—popular with WWII spies in the 20th century, and tourists needing a little break in the 21st century (nice after this walk).*

⓬ Praça dos Restauradores

This monumental square connects Rossio with Avenida da Liberdade. The obelisk at its centerpiece celebrates the restoration of

Portuguese independence from Spain in 1640 (without any help from the still-missing Sebastian mentioned earlier).

Overlooking the square is the 1920s Art Deco facade of the Eden Theater. About 100 yards farther up the boulevard (past a Metro station and TI, on the left) is the Elevador da Glória funicular that climbs to the Bairro Alto.

• *While this walk ends here, you can stroll up Avenida da Liberdade for a good look at another facet of this fine city. The next walk (Bairro Alto and Chiado Stroll) starts at the funicular just up the street on your left.*

⓭ Avenida da Liberdade

This tree-lined grand boulevard, running north from Rossio, connects the old town (where most of the sightseeing action is) with the newer upper town. Before the great earthquake, this was the city's royal promenade. After 1755, it was the grand boulevard of Pombal's new Lisbon—originally limited to the aristocracy. The present street, built in the 1880s and inspired by Paris' Champs-Elysées, is lined with banks, airline offices, nondescript office buildings...and eight noisy lanes of traffic. The grand "rotunda"—as the roundabout formally known as Marquês de Pombal is called—tops off the Avenida da Liberdade with a commanding statue of Pombal. Allegorical symbols of his impressive accomplishments decorate the statue. (A single-minded dictator can do a lot in 27 years.) Beyond that lies the fine Edward VII Park. From the Rotunda (M: Marquês de Pombal), it's an enjoyable 20-minute downhill walk along the mile-long avenue back to the Baixa.

BAIRRO ALTO AND CHIADO STROLL

The Old Word-feeling Bairro Alto ("High Town") and trendy Chiado perch just above the busy Baixa. This walk (rated ▲▲▲) connects dramatic viewpoints, leafy parks with inviting kiosk cafés, skinny streets lined with fado clubs, a dramatic church, an earthquake-toppled convent, the Chiado's trendy dining and shopping scene, and a classic coffee house.

Rise above the Baixa on the funicular called Elevador da Glória, located near the obelisk at Praça dos Restauradores (opposite the Hard Rock Café, €3.60 if you pay driver, €1.25 if zapping with Viva Viagem card, 6/hour); you can also hike up alongside the tracks.

• *Leaving the funicular on top, turn right (go 100 yards, up into a park) to enjoy the city view from the...*

❶ Miradouro de São Pedro de Alcântara (Viewpoint)

A tile map guides you through the view, which stretches from the twin towers of the cathedral (on far right, near the river), to the ramparts of the castle birthplace of Lisbon (capping the hill, on right), to another quaint, tree-topped viewpoint in Graça (directly across, end of trolley #28E), to the skyscraper towers of the new city in the distance (far left). Whenever you see a big old building in Lisbon, it's often a former convent or monastery. With the dissolution of monastic religious orders in 1834, these buildings were

LISBON

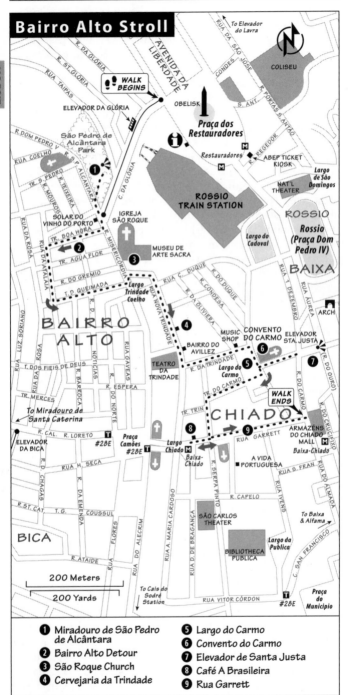

Bairro Alto Stroll

① Miradouro de São Pedro de Alcântara
② Bairro Alto Detour
③ São Roque Church
④ Cervejaria da Trindade
⑤ Largo do Carmo
⑥ Convento do Carmo
⑦ Elevador de Santa Justa
⑧ Café A Brasileira
⑨ Rua Garrett

nationalized and are now occupied by hospitals, schools, or the military.

In the park, a bust honors a 19th-century local journalist (founder of Lisbon's first daily newspaper) and a charming, barefooted delivery boy. This district is famous for its writers, poets, publishers, and bohemians.

• *Directly across the street from where you got off the Elevador da Glória is* **Solar do Vinho do Porto,** *run by the Port Wine Institute—the best place in town to sample the famous fortified wine from northern Portugal. Step inside or consider returning later for an educational tasting (for a description, see page 119).*

Next, side-trip directly across from the top of the funicular into the old grid-plan streets of the Bairro Alto.

❷ Bairro Alto Detour

The Bairro Alto, or "High Town," is one of the most characteristic and charming districts in Lisbon. Designed in the 16th century with a very modern (at the time) grid-plan layout, the district housed ship workers back when Portugal was a world power and its ships planted the Portuguese flag all around the globe. Today, the Bairro Alto is quiet in the morning, but buzzes with a thriving restaurant scene in the evening.

While it's fun to wander, follow this route for a good sampling: Go two blocks gently uphill on Travessa da Boa-Hora, turn left on Rua da Atalaia, continue three blocks, and then head left down Travessa da Queimada until you cross the big street (leaving the Bairro Alto) and reach the small square, Largo Trindade Coelho.

• *On Largo Trindade Coelho is the...*

❸ São Roque Church

Step inside and sit in a pew in the middle to take it all in (free; Mon 14:00-18:00, Tue-Sun 9:00-19:00—until 18:00 in winter, Thu until 20:00). Built in the 16th century, the ▲ church of St. Roque—dedicated to the saint who protects the faithful from disease and plagues—is one of Portugal's first Jesuit churches. The painted-wood, false-domed ceiling is perfectly flat. The acoustics here are top-notch, important in a Jesuit church, where the emphasis is on the sermon (given from twin stone pulpits midnave). The numbered panels on the floor were tombs, nameless because they were for lots of people. They're empty now—the practice was stopped in the 19th century when parishioners didn't want plague victims rotting under their feet.

Lisbon's Kiosks

The kiosk—that's *quiosque* in Portuguese—is a standard feature of squares and viewpoints all over town. These little pavilions got their start in the 19th century selling snacks and drinks. But they fell out of favor, with some being converted to newsstands or lottery sales points. Now they're back, with outdoor cafés turning parks and squares into neighborhood hangouts and meeting points. Older kiosks have been restored, and new ones are being built all the time and can be quite trendy.

Survey the rich side chapels. The highlight is the **Chapel of St. John the Baptist** (left of altar, gold and blue lapis lazuli columns). It looks like it came right out of the Vatican...because it did. Made in Rome from precious materials, the chapel was the site of one papal Mass before it was disassembled and shipped to Lisbon. Per square inch, it was the most costly chapel ever constructed in Portugal. No-  tice the mosaic floor (with the spherical symbol of Portugal) and, on the walls, three intricate, beautiful mosaics—a Vatican specialty, designed to take the place of real paintings, which were vulnerable to damage from candle smoke and incense. Notice also the delicate "sliced marble" symmetry and imagine the labor involved in so artfully cutting that stone five centuries ago.

To the right of the chapel, a glass case is filled with relics trying to grab your attention. The chapel to the left of St. John the Baptist features a riot of babies. Individual chapels—each for a different noble family—seem to be in competition. Keep in mind that the tiles are considered as extravagant as the gold leaf and silver.

To the right of the Chapel of St. John the Baptist, find the **sacristy** where, along with huge chests of drawers for vestments, you can see a series of 17th-century paintings illustrating scenes from the life of St. Frances Xavier—cofounder of the Jesuit order with St. Ignatius of Loyola.

On your way out, you might pop a coin into a rack of fake candles and power a prayer.

The São Roque Museum (to the left as you leave the church) is more interesting than your typical small church museum. It's filled with perhaps the best-presented collection of 16th- and 17th-century church art in town, and is well described in English. The church and this art, rare survivors of the 1755 earthquake, illustrate the religious passion that accompanied Portugal's Age of Discovery, with themes including the mission of the Jesuits and their response to the Reformation; devotion to relics; and devotion to the Virgin (€2.50, same hours as the church).

• *Back outside in the church square (charming WC underground), visit the statue of a friendly lottery-ticket salesman. Two lottery kiosks are nearby. Locals who buy into the* totoloto *(which, like national lotteries everywhere, is a form of taxation on gamblers that helps fund government social programs) rub the statue's well-polished ticket for good luck.*

Continue (kitty-corner left across the square) downhill along Rua Nova da Trindade, following the tram tracks. At #20 (on the left), pop into...

❹ Cervejaria da Trindade

The famous "oldest beer hall in Lisbon" is worth a visit for a look at its 19th-century tiles. The beautifully tiled main room, once a dining hall for monks, still holds the pulpit from which the Bible was read as the monks ate. After monastic orders were abolished in 1834, the monastery became a brewery—you'll notice that while the oldest tiles have Christian themes, the later ones (from around 1860) are all about the beer. Among the Portuguese beers on tap are Sagres, the standard lager; Sagres Preta, a good dark beer (like a porter); and Bohemia, which is sweet, with more alcohol. At the bar in front you can get a snack and beer, while more expensive dining is in the back (see page 118).

• *Continue down the hill. You'll pass the recommended **Bairro do Avillez**—one of several Lisbon eateries owned by celebrity chef José Avillez, who is helping to bring traditional recipes (like the ones at the* cervejaria *we just left) into the 21st century (see page 117 for more on his restaurants).*

Continue until the next intersection, where signs point left to the ruined Convento do Carmo. *Follow the inside trolley tracks downhill and to the left. Just before you reach the square, notice (on the left) the well-stocked music shop—selling (among other instruments) the unique Portuguese guitars used to perform fado music.*

You'll wind up in the leafy, inviting square called...

❺ Largo do Carmo

On this square decorated with an old fountain, lots of pigeons, and jacaranda trees from South America (with purple blossoms in June),

police officers guard the headquarters of the National Guard. Famous among residents, this was the last refuge of the dictatorial Salazar regime. The Portuguese people won their freedom in 1974, in a peaceful uprising called the Carnation Revolution. The name came when revolutionaries placed flowers in the guns of the soldiers, making it clear it was time for democracy here. For more history, see the sidebar.

• *On Largo do Carmo, check out the ruins of...*

❻ Convento do Carmo

After the convent was destroyed by the 1755 earthquake, the Marquês de Pombal directed that the delicate Gothic arches of its

church be left standing—supporting nothing but open sky—as a permanent reminder of that disastrous event. If you pay to enter, you'll see a fine memorial park in what was the nave, and (filling the former apse at the far end) a simple museum with Bronze Age and Roman artifacts, medieval royal sarcophagi, and a couple of Peruvian mummies—all explained in English (€3.50—cheapskates can do a deep knee-bend at the ticket desk, sneak a peek, and then crawl away; Mon-Sat 10:00-19:00, Oct-May until 18:00, closed Sun year-round).

• *Facing the convent, take the little lane that cuts around its right side. Head up the stairs next to the Bella Lisa Elevador restaurant to reach the gray, iron...*

❼ Elevador de Santa Justa

In 1902, an architect who had studied under Gustav Eiffel completed this 150-foot-tall iron elevator, connecting the lower and upper parts of town. The elevator's Neo-Gothic motifs are an attempt to match the ruined church near its top. It's free to peer through the railings from the entry-level ramp, but I'd spring for a ticket (€1.50) to climb the spiral stairs up to the top-floor lookout—with unobstructed views over the city. (Elevator and rooftop deck-€5;

The Carnation Revolution

António Salazar, who ruled Portugal from 1926 to 1968, was modern Europe's longest-ruling dictator (he died in 1970). Salazar's authoritarian regime, the Estado Novo, continued in power under Prime Minister Marcelo Caetano until 1974.

By the 1970s, fighting in Portugal's far-flung colonies over the previous decade had demoralized much of Salazar's military, and at home, there was a growing appetite for a modern democracy. On April 25, 1974, several prominent members of the military reluctantly sided with a growing popular movement to oust the government. Their withdrawal of support spelled the end of the Salazar era. Five people died that April day, in a well-planned, relatively bloodless coup. Citizens spilled into the streets to cheer and put flowers in soldiers' rifle barrels, giving the event its name: the Carnation Revolution. Suddenly, people were free to speak aloud what they formerly could only whisper in private.

In the revolution's aftermath, the country struggled to get the hang of democratic practices. Its economy suffered as overseas colonies fell to nationalist uprisings, flooding the country with some 800,000 immigrants. For colonial overlords, life went from "shrimp day and night" to a sudden collapse of the empire; for their own safety, they fled back to Portugal. A good number of these "returnees" didn't fit into their newly democratic old country. Feeling like people without a homeland, many ultimately left Portugal (joining Salazar's henchmen, who took refuge in Brazil). Even those who stayed were generally pro-dictator and angry about the revolution, contributing to a polarization of modern Portuguese society that exists to this day.

In 1976, the Portuguese adopted a constitution that separated church and state. These changes helped to break down an almost medieval class system and established parliamentary law. Mario Soares, a former enemy of the Salazar regime, became the new prime minister, ruling as a stabilizing presence through much of the next two decades. Today, Portugal is enthusiastically democratic.

---

also covered—without the deck—by 24-hour Viva Viagem card, or €1.25 with zapping; daily 7:00-23:00, until 22:00 in winter.)

Stroll around this celebration of the Industrial Age, enjoy the view, then retrace your steps to the square in front of the convent. (The nearby Leitaria Académica, a venerable little working-class eatery with tables spilling onto the delightful square, can be handy for a snack or drink.)

• *Continue straight up through Largo do Carmo, walking a block slightly uphill on Travessa do Carmo. At the next square, take a left on Rua Serpa Pinto, walking downhill to Rua Garrett, where—in the little*

Portugal's Greatest Poets

The Portuguese are justifiably proud of their two most famous poets, whose names, works, and memorials you may encounter in your travels.

Portugal's most important poet, **Luís de Camões** (1524-1580), was a Renaissance-age equivalent of ancient Greece's Homer. Camões' masterpiece, *The Lusiads (Os Lusíadas)*, tells the story of an explorer far from home. But instead of Odysseus, this epic poem describes the journey of Vasco da Gama, the man who found the route from Europe to India. Camões—who had sailed to Morocco to fight the Moors (where he lost an eye), to Goa (where he was imprisoned for debt), and to China (where he was shipwrecked)—was uniquely qualified to write about Portugal's pursuit of empire on the high seas. For more on Camões, see page 70.

Fernando Pessoa (1888-1935) used multiple personas in

his poetry. He'd take on the voice of a simple countryman and express his love of nature in free verse. Or he'd write as an erudite scholar, sharing philosophical thoughts in a more formal style. By varying his voice, he was able to more easily explore different viewpoints and truths. While Pessoa loved the classics—reading Milton, Byron, Shelley, and Poe—he was a true 20th-century bohemian at heart. Café A Brasileira, where he'd often meet with friends, has a statue of Pessoa outside. Today, fado musicians still remember Pessoa, paying homage to him by putting his poetry into the Portuguese version of the blues.

pedestrian zone 50 yards uphill on the right—you'll find a famous old café across from the Baixa-Chiado Metro stop.

❽ Café A Brasileira

Slinky with Art Nouveau decor, this café is a 100-year-old institution for coffeehouse junkies. A Brasileira was originally a shop selling Brazilian products, a reminder that this has long been the city's shopping zone. Drop in for a *bica* (Lisbon slang for an espresso) or a *pingado* (with a dollop of steamed milk; either costs €0.70 at the bar). A *pastel de nata* custard tart costs just €1.30—but the

best place in town for one is just a short walk away (see "Exploring More of the Bairro Alto," later). WCs are down the stairs near the entrance.

The statue out front is of the poet **Fernando Pessoa** (see sidebar), making him a perpetual regular at this café. He was the literary and creative soul of Lisbon in the 1920s and 1930s, when the country's avant-garde poets, writers, and painters would hang out here.

At the neighboring **Baixa-Chiado Metro stop,** a slick series of escalators whisks people effortlessly between Chiado Square and the Baixa. It's a free and fun way to survey a long, long line of Portuguese—but for now, we'll stay in the Chiado neighborhood. (If you'll be coming for fado in the evening—recommended places are nearby—consider getting here by zipping up the escalator.)

• *The Chiado district is popular for its shopping and theaters. Browse downhill on...*

❾ Rua Garrett

As you stroll, notice the mosaic sidewalks, ironwork balconies, and fine shops. The street lamps you see are decorated with the sym-

bol of Lisbon: a ship, carrying the remains of St. Vincent, guarded by two ravens.

As you walk, peek into classy stores, such as the fabric-lover's paradise **Paris em Lisboa**—imagine how this would have been the ultimate in *oh là là* fashion in the 19th century (at #77, on the right). The next cross street, Rua Serpa Pinto, leads (in one block) to the **São Carlos Theater**—Lisbon's opera house. Celebrity chef José Avillez, whose eatery we passed earlier, and his culinary rivals have revitalized this sleepy quarter with several restaurants. (Avillez's Belcanto has often appeared high on the list of the "50 Best Restaurants in the World.") Between here and the theater is the recommended **Loja da Burel,** selling traditional and modern Portuguese woolens (see "Shopping in Lisbon").

Continuing along Rua Garrett, at the next corner (after the church, at #73) is the venerable **Bertrand** bookstore—with English books and a good guidebook selection. **A Vida Portuguesa**—my favorite shop for Portuguese gifts (quality textiles, soaps, home decor, sardines, wine, and so on) is at the end of the street behind the bookstore (daily 10:00-20:00, Rua Anchieta 11).

Along the main drag, you'll start to see more and more international chains before Rua Garrett ends abruptly at the entrance of the big **Armazéns do Chiado mall.** This grand, six-floor shopping center connects Lisbon's lower and upper towns with a world of ways to spend money (including a handy food court on the sixth floor). For Italian-style gelato, locals like **Santini em Casa,** a few steps downhill to the left as you face the mall (at #9).

• *This walk is over. Whether you leave the Bairro Alto or stay to explore, directions are below.*

   Leaving the Bairro Alto: *To get from the mall to the Baixa—the lower town—take the elevator (press 1) down to the ground level. To get from the mall to the Metro, exit through the lowest floor of the mall, turn right, and walk 50 yards to the Baixa-Chiado Metro stop.*

   Or, if you have time and interest, consider...

Exploring More of the Bairro Alto

A short walk from the mall gives you a more complete look at this high-altitude neighborhood and a scenic viewpoint. Backtrack (heading west) up Rua Garrett to the square **Praça Luís de Camões,** where the great writer stands on a pillar, leaning on a sword—more warrior than poet.

Behind Camões, bear west along Rua do Loreto. Just where the square and street meet, on the right at #2, notice the hubbub at the recommended **Manteigaria**—the best spot in town for a *pastel de nata* custard tart. Even if it looks crowded, you'll typically get served quickly (cashiers come along the line to take your order). Pastry in hand, shimmy down the narrow hall inside, where you can stand at the counter and watch the pastry chefs in action—perpetually cutting cross-sections of delicate dough, pressing it into little tins, filling the pastries with gooey custard, and popping big trays into the oven (at 750 degrees Fahr-

enheit, to get just the right amount of caramelizing on top). Be sure to sprinkle your piping-hot pastry with powdered sugar and cinnamon.

   Continue three more blocks on Rua do Loreto, passing the picturesque **Elevador da Bica funicular.**

Then, one block farther, turn left on Rua Marechal Saldanha to reach the **Miradouro de Santa Catarina** (a.k.a. the "Bica mirador"), a terrace—flanked by bars—that overlooks the city's harbor and river. This is a popular hangout for the dreadlocked granola crowd on a balmy evening. You'll see a monument to the Cape of Good Hope (a.k.a. the Cape of Torment) that personifies the cape as a monster. This mythic treatment was popularized by poet Camões' *The Lusiads,* which celebrated and nearly deified the great explorers of Portugal's Age of Discovery (such as Vasco da Gama, portrayed as Ulysses), who had to overcome such demons in their conquest of the sea.

Sights in Lisbon

CENTRAL LISBON

To get a full picture of the best of central Lisbon, take the three neighborhood walks (covering the Bairro Alto, Alfama, and Baixa; see earlier). Several central Lisbon sights are described in detail in those self-guided walks: São Jorge Castle, the Museum and School of Portuguese Decorative Arts, and the Fado Museum (in "Alfama Stroll and the Castle"), and the São Roque Church and Museum (in "Bairro Alto and Chiado Stroll").

▲Lisbon Cathedral (Sé de Lisboa)

The cathedral, just a few blocks east of Praça do Comércio, is not much on the inside, but its fortress-like exterior—solid enough to survive the 1755 earthquake—is a textbook example of the stark and powerful Romanesque "fortress of God" so typical of its age. Twin, castle-like, crenellated towers solidly frame an impressive rose window.

Cost and Hours: Free, Tue-Sat 9:00-19:00, Sun-Mon until 17:00. You can pay extra to visit the cloister (€2.50, closed Sun) and treasury (€2.50)—but I'd skip them. It's on Largo da Sé, several blocks east of the Baixa—take Rua da Conceição east, which turns into Rua de Santo António da Sé. Trolleys #12E and #28E stop right out front, where the square is clogged with tuk-tuks offering tours around town.

Visiting the Church: Started in 1150, this was the first place of worship that Christians built after they retook Lisbon from the Moors. Located on the former site of a mosque, it made a powerful statement: The Reconquista was here to stay. The church is also the site of the 1195 baptism of St. Anthony—a favorite saint of Portugal (locals appeal to him for help in finding a parking spot, true love, and lost objects). Naturally for Portugal, tile panels around the baptismal font (in the back-left corner) portray St. Anthony preaching to the fish. Also, some of St. Vincent is buried here—

António Salazar

Q: What do you get when you cross a lawyer, an economist, and a dictator?

A: António Salazar, who was all three—a dictator who ruled Portugal through harsh laws and a strict budget that hurt the poor.

Shortly after a 1926 military coup "saved" Portugal's floundering democracy from itself, General Oscar Carmona appointed António de Olivei-ra Salazar (1889-1970) as finance minister. A former professor of economics and law at the University of Coimbra, Salazar balanced the budget and the interests of the country's often-warring factions. His skill and his repu-tation as a clean-living, fair-minded patriot earned him a promotion. In 1932, he became prime minister, and he set about creating his New State (Estado Novo).

For nearly four decades, Salazar ruled a stable but isolated nation by harmonizing the traditional power blocs of the ruling class—the military, big business, large landowners, and the Catholic Church. He enforced his Christian fascism with the backing of the military—and his secret police.

As a person, Salazar was respected, but not loved. The son of a farm manager, he originally studied to be a priest be-fore going on to become a scholar and writer. He never mar-ried. Quiet, low-key, and unassuming, he attended church reg-ularly and lived a nonmaterialistic existence. But when faced with opposition, he was ruthless, and his secret police became an object of fear and hatred.

Salazar steered Portugal through the turmoil of Spain's Civil War (1936-1939), remaining officially neutral while secret-ly supporting Franco's fascists. He detested Nazi Germany's "pagan" leaders, but respected Mussolini for reconciling with the pope. In World War II, Portugal was officially neutral, but was often friendly with longtime ally Britain and used as a base for espionage. After the war, Salazar's regime benefited great-ly from the United States' Marshall Plan for economic recovery (which Spain missed out on during Franco's rule). The country joined NATO in 1949.

Salazar distracted his poor and isolated masses with a cynical credo: "*Fado, Fátima, and Futebol*" (the three "Fs"). Salazar was undone by two factors: the liberal 1960s and the unpopular, draining wars Portugal fought abroad to try to keep its colonial empire intact. When Salazar died in 1970, the regime that followed became increasingly less credible, lead-ing to the liberating events of the Carnation Revolution in 1974 (see "The Carnation Revolution" sidebar, earlier).

legend has it that in the 12th century, his remains were brought to Lisbon on a ship guarded by two sacred black ravens, the symbol of the city. Take a stroll through the vast, dark interior—with rounded arches and a dim, windowless nave, it's quintessentially Romanesque. Near the altar, the darkness gives way to a slightly lighter Gothic zone. Here you can choose to pay to enter the ambulatory and peaceful **cloister** (an archaeological work-in-progress—they're currently uncovering Roman ruins). The humble **treasury,** back near the entrance, is worth its fee only if you want to support the church and climb some stairs.

▲Aljube Museum of Resistance and Freedom (Museu do Aljube)

This new museum is the best place to learn about Portugal's troubled mid-20th century. It fills a stern building called the **Aljube** (from a Moorish word meaning "waterless well"), immediately behind the cathedral. Once a Muslim prison, then a jail during the Inquisition (and on a site that dates back to Roman times), the Aljube later became the main political prison of Portugal's fascist regime under António Salazar. Today, it houses a modern, well-presented, three-floor exhibit detailing Salazar's rise to power, the creation of the Estado Novo, crimes against the Portuguese people, and the eventual end of the regime with the 1974 Carnation Revolution. Exhibits tell the story (in English) with photos and subtitled video clips, as well as some original documents and other artifacts. While often overshadowed by Franco in Spain and the communist regimes of eastern Europe, Salazar was hardly a Boy Scout—and this long-overdue museum documents his abuses. It fills a much-needed gap for those with an appetite for recent history.

Cost and Hours: €3, free Sun before 13:00, open Tue-Sun 10:00-18:00, closed Mon, Rua de Augusto Rosa 42, tel. 218-172-400, www.museudoaljube.pt. The entrance is tucked under a tall staircase, on a little square with a stop for trolleys #12E and #28E, between the cathedral and the Alfama.

Elevador de Santa Justa

This 150-foot-tall iron tower, built in 1902, connects the flat Baixa district with the Bairro Alto/Chiado districts up above. One of the city's main landmarks, it offers a sweat-free connection to the upper town, as well as a fine city view up top. You can climb to the rooftop lookout alone (and skip the elevator ride) if you're already in the Bairro Alto/Chiado.

During busy times, the long line (which wraps up the stairs and around behind the elevator's base) moves slowly. If it's backed up, skip it or come back at a quieter time. Two much faster routes up to Chiado are nearby: the elevators inside Armazéns do Chiado mall, or the escalators inside the Baixa-Chiado Metro station (see "Ways to Get from the Baixa Up to the Bairro Alto and Chiado," page 19).

Cost and Hours: Elevator—€5 (round-trip tickets only), rooftop view deck—€1.50; free with 24-hour Viva Viagem card or €1.25 with zapping; departures every 10 minutes, daily 7:00-23:00, until 22:00 in winter, http://carris.transporteslisboa.pt.

NORTH LISBON

A visit to this North Lisbon sight can be combined with sightseeing in Belém, a quick €8 taxi ride away.

▲▲Gulbenkian Museum (Museu Calouste Gulbenkian)

This is the best of Lisbon's 40 museums, and it's worth the trip for art lovers (two miles north of the city center). Calouste Gulbenki-

an (1869-1955), an Armenian oil tycoon, gave Portugal his art collection (or "harem," as he called it) in gratitude for the hospitable asylum granted him in Lisbon during World War II (where he lived from 1942 until his death). The Portuguese consider Gulbenkian an inspirational model of how to be thoughtfully wealthy: He made a habit of "tithing for art," spending 10 percent of his income on things of beauty, and his billion-dollar estate is still a vital arts foundation promoting culture in Portugal. The foundation/museum, with its classy modern building set in a delightful garden, often hosts classical music concerts in the museum's auditoriums.

Gulbenkian's wide-ranging collection, spanning 5,000 years of European, Egyptian, Islamic, and Asian art, offers the most purely enjoyable museum-going experience in Iberia—it's both educational and just plain beautiful. Art Nouveau fans should take note of the museum's stunning Lalique jewelry collection. The Gulbenkian is cool, uncrowded, gorgeously lit, and easy to grasp, displaying only a few select and exquisite works from each epoch. Walk through five millennia of human history, appreciating our ancestors by seeing objects they treasured.

Cost and Hours: €10, includes main branch and Modern Collection (located across park; see later), free on Sun after 14:00; open Wed-Mon 10:00-18:00, closed Tue; pleasant gardens, good air-conditioned cafeteria; Berna 45, tel. 217-823-000, www.museu.gulbenkian.pt.

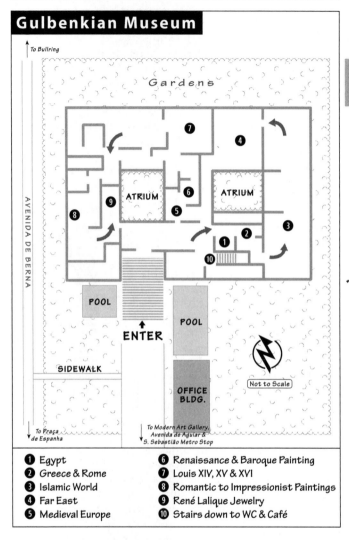

Gulbenkian Museum

To Bullring

Gardens

LISBON

AVENIDA DE BERNA

To Bullring

ATRIUM

ATRIUM

❼

❹

❻

❾

❺

❽

❸

❷

❶

❿

POOL

POOL

ENTER

SIDEWALK

Not to Scale

OFFICE BLDG.

To Praça de Espanha

To Modern Art Gallery, Avenida de Aguiar & S. Sebastião Metro Stop

❶ Egypt
❷ Greece & Rome
❸ Islamic World
❹ Far East
❺ Medieval Europe

❻ Renaissance & Baroque Painting
❼ Louis XIV, XV & XVI
❽ Romantic to Impressionist Paintings
❾ René Lalique Jewelry
❿ Stairs down to WC & Café

Getting There: From downtown, hop a cab (€7) or take the Metro from Restauradores to the São Sebastião stop; leave the platform by following *Avenida de Aguiar (norte)* signs. Then, to leave the station, follow signs to *Avenida de Aguiar (nascente)*. Once at street level, it's about a five-minute walk: Go a long block downhill on Avenida de Aguiar with the massive El Corte Inglés department store behind you. Just before the roundabout (across from the funky, pink Spanish embassy on the left), you'll see a small sign pointing right to the *fundação*—the museum entrance is up the stairs and straight ahead through this park, past a long concrete office building, about 100 yards away.

The Gulbenkian's **Modern Collection (Coleção Moderna)** is a five-minute walk from the main branch: Go straight ahead from the main door, and take the path through the park on your left just before the busy road.

◐ **Self-Guided Tour:** From the entrance lobby, there are two wings, covering roughly pre-1500 and post-1500. Following the museum's mostly chronological layout, you'll pass through the following sections:

❶ **Egypt** (2500-500 B.C.): Ancient Egyptians, believing that life really began after death, carved statues to preserve the memory of the deceased, whether it be a prince (*Statue of the Official Bes*, 660-610 B.C., with an inscription calling him "the king's friend") or a family pet. The cat statue nurses her kittens atop a coffin that once held the cat's mummy, preserved for the afterlife. Egyptians honored cats—even giving them gold earrings (notice this statue's ears are pierced). They believed cats helped the goddess Bastet keep watch over the household. Now, thousands of years later, we remember the Egyptians for these sturdy, dignified statues, built for eternity.

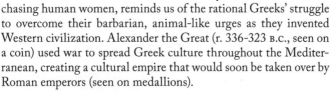

❷ **Greece and Rome** (500 B.C.-A.D. 500): The black-and-red Greek vase (calyx-crater), decorated with scenes of half-human satyrs chasing human women, reminds us of the rational Greeks' struggle to overcome their barbarian, animal-like urges as they invented Western civilization. Alexander the Great (r. 336-323 B.C., seen on a coin) used war to spread Greek culture throughout the Mediterranean, creating a cultural empire that would soon be taken over by Roman emperors (seen on medallions).

Journey even further back in time to Mesopotamia (modern Iraq) and the very roots of civilization. The Assyrian relief of Ashurnasirpal II (884-859 B.C.) evokes this distant culture, which invented writing.

❸ **Islamic World** (700-1500): The Muslims who lived in Portugal—as far west of Mecca as you could get back then—might have decorated their homes with furnishings from all over the Islamic world. Imagine a Moorish sultan, dressed in a shirt from Syria, sitting on a carpet from Persia in a courtyard with Moroccan tiles. By a bubbling fountain, he puffs on a hookah.

The culture of Moorish Iberia (711-1492) was among Europe's most sophisticated after the Fall of Rome. The intricate patterns on the glass mosque lamps (behind the partition on the left) are

collection of furniture, as well as paintings by renowned European masters such as Hieronymus Bosch, Jan van Eyck, and Raphael—all in a grand palace that's sleekly renovated and well-presented.

Cost and Hours: €6, free first Sun of month; open Tue-Sun 10:00-18:00, closed Mon; good cafeteria with shaded garden seating that overlooks the river, Rua das Janeles Verdes 9, tel. 213-912-800, www.museudearteantiga.pt.

Getting There: It's about a mile west of downtown Lisbon. From Praça da Figueira, take trolley #15E to Cais Rocha, cross the street, and walk up a lot of steps. To stop right in front, take bus #714 from either Praça da Figueira or Praça do Comércio. Note that trolley #15E and bus #714 both continue to the sights in Belém; if you have time when returning at the end of your Belém day and aren't museumed out, this is a handy choice.

Visiting the Museum: Here are some of the museum's highlights, starting on the top floor. (But note that a planned renovation in 2017 may cause some changes.) From the ticket desk, turn right to find the elevator and press button 2.

Top Floor, Portuguese Painting and Sculpture: From the elevator, veer right through the atrium and find the big, red room at the far end. *The Panels of St. Vincent* are a multipart altarpiece by the late-15th-century master Nuno Gonçalves. A gang of 60 real people—everyone from royalty to sailors and beggars—surrounds Lisbon's patron saint. Of note is the only recognized portrait of Prince Henry the Navigator, responsible for setting Portugal on the path to exploration. Find him in the middle—an elder gentleman dressed in black with a wide-brimmed hat, hands together almost in prayer.

Explore the rest of the floor: Head back into the atrium, turn right, then turn right again into the long room. If you've visited the sights in Belém, you'll recognize the Monastery of Jerónimos before it was fully decorated (1657 painting by Felipe Lobo). Two rooms away, find an exceptional portrait of the baby-faced King Sebastian—who died young when he led an incursion into Africa. The armor is typical of Iberia for the era, as is the royal jaw and pursed lips caused by Habsburg inbreeding.

Before you head down the stairs (in the middle of the atrium) to the next floor, notice the statue of a pregnant Mary (*The Virgin of Expectation*, c. 1340-1350). This unusual theme was common in rural parts of Portugal (such as the Alentejo, the close-to-the-ground region in the southeast), where the Virgin's fertility was her most persuasive quality in recruiting local followers.

Middle Floor, Art from the Portuguese Discoveries: This floor collects items that Portuguese explorers brought home from their far-flung travels. Coming down the stairs, bear left, then right, to find the room with large, enchanting Namban screen paintings (*Namban,* meaning "southern barbarians," the catch-all term the Japanese applied to all foreigners). These show the Portuguese from a 16th-century Japanese perspective—with long noses, dark complexions, and great skill at climbing rigging, like acrobats. The Portuguese, the first Europeans to make contact with Japan, gave the Japanese guns, Catholicism (Nagasaki was founded by Portuguese Jesuits), and a new deep-frying technique we now know as tempura.

Now do a counterclockwise circle around this floor, stocked with furniture, large vases, ivory carvings, fine china, and ceramics. Imagine how astonishing these treasures must have seemed when the early explorers returned with them. Facing the atrium are some beautiful tiles from Damascus—a gift from Calouste Gulbenkian (founder of the Gulbenkian Museum listed above). Eventually you reach a treasury of gold and silver items. Look for the freestanding glass case with a gorgeous golden monstrance, with its carrying case displayed just behind it—the bejeweled Rococo Communion-host holder was made for Lisbon's Bemposta Palace. Farther along is the even more exquisite  Monstrance of Belém, commissioned by Manuel I and made from East African tribute gold brought back by Vasco da Gama. Squint at the fine enamel creatures filling a tide pool on the base, the 12 apostles gathered around the glass case for the Communion wafer (the fancy top pops off), and the white dove hanging like a mobile under the all-powerful God bidding us peace on earth.

Heading back to the atrium, don't miss the small, dimly lit room (on the left) displaying an impressive jewelry collection, including pieces decorated with the red cross of the affluent Order of Christ, whose members helped plan and fund Portuguese explorations.

Back in the atrium, before continuing downstairs, stop to admire a 17th-century painting of Lisbon before the 1755 earthquake. Notice the royal palace on Praça do Comércio and the ship-clogged Rio Tejo.

Ground Floor, European Paintings: Pass through the gift shop, veer left, and follow the one-way route through paintings from all over Europe. A few rooms in, note the larger-than-life paintings of the twelve apostles by the Spanish master Zurburán.

Continue to the end of the hall, then find the room with Bosch's *Temptations of St. Anthony* (a three-paneled altarpiece fantasy, c. 1500) and Albrecht Dürer's *St. Jerome*. St. Jerome—you'll see other portraits of him in this collection, always with a skull—is all-important to Lisbon as the primary figure behind the Monastery of Jerónimos in Belém. Finally, exit through the few remnants of the palace. Note the Pombal coat-of-arms that decorates the elaborate, Baroque doorway (find the star); the palace was originally purchased by the brother of the powerful Marquês de Pombal.

BELÉM DISTRICT

About five miles west of downtown Lisbon, the Belém district is a stately pincushion of important sights from Portugal's Golden Age, when Vasco da Gama and company turned the country into Europe's wealthiest power. Belém was the sending-off point for voyages in the Age of Discovery. Before embarking, sailors would stay and pray at the Monastery of Jerónimos, and when they returned, the Belém Tower welcomed them home. The grand buildings of Belém survived the great 1755 earthquake, so this is the best place to experience the Manueline architectural style (see sidebar on page 73). After the earthquake, safety-conscious (and rattled) royalty chose to live here—in wooden rather than stone buildings. The modern-day president of Portugal calls Belém home.

To celebrate the 300th anniversary of independence from Spain, a grand exhibition was held here in 1940, resulting in fine parks, fountains, and monuments.

Getting to Belém: You have multiple options: By **taxi** or **Uber,** figure no more than about 20 minutes and €10 from downtown. **Buses** #714 and #728 serve Belém, and the coastal train line running from Lisbon's **Cais do Sodré station** gets you there in about 10 minutes.

But if you have the time, I prefer riding the slower **trolley #15E** (30-40 minutes, catch at Praça da Figueira or Praça do Comércio). In Belém, the first trolley stop is at the National Coach Museum (stop is called simply "Belém"—you'll see the brown sign for *Museu dos Coches* just before the stop); the second stop (Belém-Jerónimos) is at the Monastery of Jerónimos; and another (Pedrouços) is two stops farther, at a little square two blocks inland from the Belém Tower. Even if you miss the first stop, you can't miss the second stop at the massive monastery.

Planning Your Time: Nearly all of Belém's museums are closed on Monday (though the Monument to the Discoveries is open Mon May-Sept). And be aware that the sights can be mobbed by cruise travelers in the morning.

Consider doing Belém's sights from east to west, in the order

LISBON

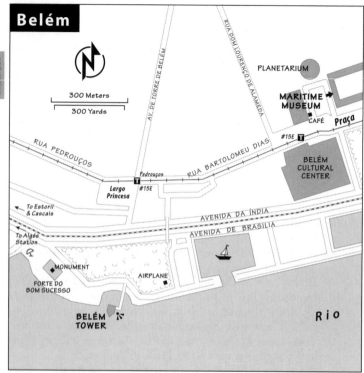

you'll reach them from the tram or train: the National Coach Museum, pastry and coffee break, Monastery of Jerónimos, Maritime Museum (if interested) and/or lunch at its cafeteria (public access, museum entry not required), Monument to the Discoveries, and Belém Tower. If arriving by taxi, you could start at Belém Tower—the farthest point—and do the recommended lineup in reverse, ending at the National Coach Museum (which has easier public transit connections than the tower). Belém also has a cultural center, a children's museum, and a planetarium—not priorities for a quick visit. For recommended eateries in this area, see page 67.

Returning to Downtown: When you're through, hop on trolley #15E or bus #714 to return to Praça da Figueira or Praça do Comércio, or ride the coastal train back to Cais do Sodré. If you have time and energy left, you could hop off the trolley or bus to tour the Museum of Ancient Art on the way home (see page 60). Bus #728 takes you to Santa Apolónia station, and continues to Parque das Nações and Oriente station.

Tourist Information: A little TI kiosk is directly across the street from the entrance to the monastery (Tue-Sat 10:00-13:00 & 14:00-18:00, closed Sun-Mon, tel. 213-658-437).

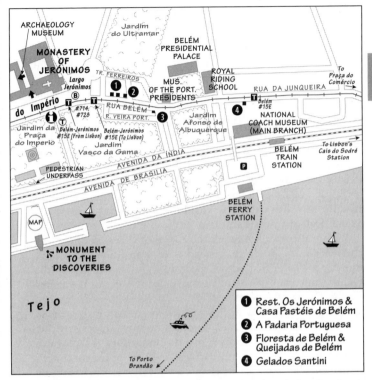

LISBON

1 Rest. Os Jerónimos & Casa Pastéis de Belém

2 A Padaria Portuguesa

3 Floresta de Belém & Queijadas de Belém

4 Gelados Santini

▲▲National Coach Museum (Museu Nacional dos Coches)

In 1905, the last queen of Portugal saw that cars would soon obliterate horse-drawn carriages as a form of transportation. She decided to preserve her fine collection of royal coaches, which became today's National Coach Museum. The impressive collection is split between two buildings, each with its own ticket. The main branch—in a huge, blocky, concrete building closer to the river—has the bulk of

the collection, with 70 dazzling coaches, all described in English. The Royal Riding School, closer to the tram tracks, is a historical space with a gorgeous interior but only about a half-dozen coaches on display. If you want to really appreciate the coaches themselves, focus on the main branch. But to see regal spaces (which are rare in Lisbon), add on the Royal Riding School.

Cost and Hours: Main branch—€6, Royal Riding School—€4, €8 combo-ticket covers both, free first Sun of month, open Tue-Sun 10:00-18:00, closed Mon, tel. 213-610-850, www. museudoscoches.pt.

Visiting the Main Branch: The museum is right across the street from the Belém tram stop (on one side) and the Belém train station (on the other). Find the steps down directly to the ticket office under the building, then ride an elevator up to the collection, where you'll loop through two rooms.

The first coach dates from around 1600. This crude and simple vehicle was once used by Philip II, king of Spain and Portugal, to shuttle between Madrid and Lisbon. Notice that the coach has no driver's seat—its drivers would actually ride the horses. You'll have to trust me on this, but if you lift up the cushion from the passengers' seat, you'll find a potty hole—also handy for road sickness. Imagine how slow and rough the ride would be with bad roads and a crude leather-strap suspension.

From here, walk through the historical collection, displayed chronologically. Study the evolution of suspension technology, starting with the first coach, made in the 15th century in the Hungarian town of Kocs (pronounced "coach"—hence the name). By the 17th century—when this collection begins—coaches had caught on in a big way in Portugal, which was an early adopter. Trace the improvements made through the next century, noticing that as the decoration increases, so does the comfort. A Portuguese coat of arms indicates that a carriage was part of the royal fleet. Ornamentation often includes a folk festival of exotic faces from Portugal's distant colonies.

In the middle of the hall shines the lumbering Oceans Coach, as ornate as it is long. At the stern, gold figures symbolize the Atlantic and Indian Oceans holding hands, a reminder of Portugal's mastery of the sea. The Oceans Coach is flanked by two equally stunning coaches with similar symbols of ocean exploration. These were part of a thematic convoy sent by King João V to Pope Clement XI in 1716.

Next you'll see the Exchange of the Princesses carriages, which were used for a ceremonial procession to the Portuguese-Spanish border to swap royal kids for marriage (to shore up the two kingdoms' diplomatic relations after Portugal's 1640 independence). At the far end of the hall, peek inside the Table coach, which must have been a cozy place to hang out and wait for the exchange.

The next room organizes its carriages by theme. First you'll see "Berlins"—a new coach type (pioneered in that city, in the late 17th century) that suspended the main compartment on thick leather straps to improve the ride. You'll see ecclesiastical coaches (suggesting the high status of clergy); single-horse chaise and cabriolet coaches (including some sleek, black leather, 19th-century, Sherlock Holmes-style ones); hunting vehicles; sedan chairs;

Eating in Belém

You'll find snack bars at Belém Tower, a cafeteria at the Maritime Museum, and fun little restaurants along Rua de Belém, between the National Coach Museum and the monastery. Here are a few other eateries worth checking out:

$$ Restaurante Os Jerónimos is a busy little place good for fresh fish, where hardworking Carlos treats his customers well and serves fine, affordable meals and a fish-of-the-day special (Sun-Fri 12:00-21:30, closed Sat, Rua de Belém 74, tel. 213-638-423, next to renowned Casa Pastéis de Belém pastry café, see page 68).

$ A Padaria Portuguesa, a respected fast-food chain with fine fresh-baked bread, hearty sandwiches, and salads, is next door at #46 (daily 7:30-20:00).

Restaurant Row: Many more fine places with outdoor seating are in the restaurant row beyond the McDonald's facing the park, including **$$ Floresta de Belém,** the local favorite for their home-style Portuguese cooking, such as tasty grilled sardines and *feijoada* bean stew. They have minimal seating inside, but two cozy terraces outside (closed Sun dinner, all day Mon, and Sept; Praça Afonso de Albuquerque 1A, tel. 213-636-307). Next door, **$$ Queijadas de Belém** is a good bet for its salads, sardines, and outside seating (daily, Rua de Belém 1, tel. 213-630-034).

Dessert: In addition to the original *pastel de Belém* place (**Casa Pastéis de Belém,** described on page 68), **Gelados Santini**—a local favorite for gelato—is across the street from the National Coach Museum.

scaled-down play carriages for kids who had everything; and mail coaches. You'll also see the "Landau of the Regicide"—the coach in which King Carlos I and his heir were shot and killed on February 1, 1908. You can still see the bullet holes. (This carriage is sometimes on loan to a countryside branch; if it's not here, you'll see a model instead, with a video telling the story.)

Visiting the Royal Riding School: You'll find this regal building along the trolley tracks through Belém, kitty-corner from the main museum. The elegant old riding room with its dramatically painted ceiling is as remarkable as the carriages. Under that ceiling, you'll see a handful of fine specimens (but if you've already been to the main branch, this is a rerun). Wander upstairs to get a glimpse of velvet-covered saddles and special riding gear designed for the royal kids. A spectacular view of the entire building interior is picture-perfect (no flash). The portrait gallery covering most of Portugal's royalty is handy for putting a face to all the movers and shakers you've read about so far.

Nearby: Just past the Royal Riding School, on the landscaped hill behind the wall, is the stately, pink **Belém Palace**—the residence of Portugal's president. The palace interior is tourable only on Saturdays (€5, most tours in Portuguese), but if you're fascinated by Portuguese history, you can drop in anytime at the modern little **Museum of the Portuguese Presidents** (Museu da Presidência da República). It offers a little lesson on each of Portugal's democracy-era presidents (since 1910) and lots of state gifts (€2.50, Tue-Sun 10:00-18:00, closed Mon, look for entrance just west of Royal Riding School and palace gate).

▲Casa Pastéis de Belém

The Casa Pastéis de Belém café is the birthplace of the wonderful custard tart that's called *pastel de nata* throughout Portugal, but here it's dubbed *pastel de Belém*. You can explore this sprawling temple to Portugal's beloved custard tart like a museum, with a peek at the bakery in the rear. Since 1837, residents have been coming to this café to get their tarts fresh. Its popularity stems mainly from the fact that their recipe is a closely guarded secret—supposedly only three people know the exact proportions of the ingredients. While the recipe is fine, my hunch is that their undeniable goodness is simply because the café cranks out 20,000 or so a day—you get them fresh and crunchy, literally hot out of the oven. (Take one back to your hotel and eat it tonight and it'll taste just like any other in town.) Sit down and enjoy one with a *café com leite*. Sprinkle on as much cinnamon and powdered sugar as you like.

Tarts are €1 whether you eat in or carry out. There's often a line for take-away, but it moves quickly (pay, then take your receipt to the mob at the counter to claim your tart). If the line is extremely long, consider finding a table inside the café, which may have faster service (daily 8:00-24:00, Rua de Belém 84, tel. 213-637-423).

▲▲▲Monastery of Jerónimos

This giant, white limestone church and monastery stretches for 300 impressive yards along the Belém waterfront. King Manuel (who ruled from 1495) erected it as a "thank you" for the discoveries made by early Portuguese explorers. It was financed in part with "pepper money," a 5 percent tax on spices brought back from India. Manuel built the church near the site of a humble chapel where sailors spent their last night ashore in prayer before embarking on frightening voyages. What is the style of Manuel's church? Manueline.

Cost and Hours: Church—free, cloister—€10, includes audioguide, €12 combo-ticket with Belém Tower (cloister and tower are free on first Sun of month); monastery open Tue-Sun 10:00-18:30, Oct-April until 17:30, closed Mon year-round, www.mosteirojeronimos.pt. There's often a long line to visit the cloister,

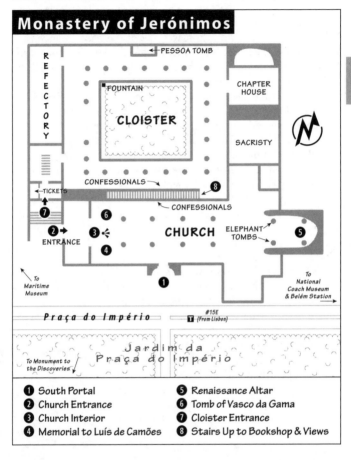

Monastery of Jerónimos

REFECTORY

← PESSOA TOMB

FOUNTAIN

CHAPTER HOUSE

CLOISTER

SACRISTY

CONFESSIONALS →

8

← TICKETS

CONFESSIONALS

7

6

2 → ENTRANCE

3

CHURCH

ELEPHANT TOMBS

5

4

To Maritime Museum

To National Coach Museum & Belém Station

1

South Portal

Praça do Império

#15E (From Lisbon)

Jardim da Praça do Império

To Monument to the Discoveries

1 South Portal
2 Church Entrance
3 Church Interior
4 Memorial to Luís de Camões
5 Renaissance Altar
6 Tomb of Vasco da Gama
7 Cloister Entrance
8 Stairs Up to Bookshop & Views

but you can cut through it to get immediately to the church entrance.

Background: As you circle around the complex, ponder the great history of this serene place. Monks often accompanied the sailor-pirates on their trading/pillaging trips, hoping to convert the heathens to Christianity. Many expeditions were financed by the Order of Christ, a brotherhood of soldier-monks. (The monks who inhabited this cloister were Hieronymites—followers of St. Jerome, hence the monastery name of Jerónimos.)

King Manuel, who did so much to promote exploration, was also the man who forcibly expelled all Jews from the country. (In 1497, the Spanish *Reyes Católicos*—Ferdinand and Isabel—agreed to allow him to marry one of their daughters on the condition that he deport the Jews.) Francis Xavier, a founder of the Spanish Jesuit order, did much of his missionary work traveling in Asia in the service of Portugal.

It was a time of extreme Christian faith. The sheer size of this religious complex is a testament to the religious motivation that—along with money—propelled the Age of Discovery.

⊘ Self-Guided Tour: Start outside the monastery:

❶ South Portal: The fancy portal, facing the street, is textbook Manueline. Henry the Navigator stands between the doors with the king's patron saint, St. Jerome (above on the left, with the lion). Henry (Manuel's uncle) built the original sailors' chapel on this site. This door is only used when Mass lets out or for Saturday weddings. (The electronic snapping sound you hear is designed to keep the pigeons away.)

• *To the left of the portal is the...*

❷ Church Entrance: As you approach the main entrance, the church is on your right and the cloister is straight ahead. Flanking the church door are kneeling statues of King Manuel I, the Fortunate (left of door, with St. Jerome), and his Spanish wife, María (right, with John the Baptist).

❸ Church Interior: The Manueline style is on the cusp of the Renaissance. The space is more open than earlier medieval churches. Slender, palm-tree-like columns don't break the interior space (as Gothic columns would), and the ceiling is all one height. Motifs from the sea hide in the decor. The sea brought Portugal 16th-century wealth and power, making this art possible. You'll see rope-like arches, ships, and monsters that evoke the mystery of undiscovered lands. Artichokes, eaten for their vitamin C to fend off scurvy, remind us of the hardships sailors faced at sea.

• *On your right as you face the altar is the...*

❹ Memorial to Luís de Camões: Camões (kah-MOISH, 1524-1580) is Portugal's Shakespeare and Casanova rolled into one, an adventurer and writer whose heroic poems, glorifying the nation's sailing exploits, live on today. It was Camões who described Portugal as the place "where land ends and the sea begins."

After college at Coimbra, Camões was banished from the court (1546) for flirting with the noble lady Dona Caterina. He lost an eye soldiering in Morocco (he's always portrayed squinting), served jail time for brawling with a bureaucrat, and then caught a ship to India and China, surviving a shipwreck on the way. While

serving as a colonial administrator in India, he plugged away at the epic poem that would become his masterpiece. Returning to Portugal, he published *The Lusiads* (*Os Lusíadas*, 1572), winning minor recognition and a small pension.

The long poem describes Vasco da Gama's first voyage to India in heroic terms, on the scale of Homer's *Odyssey*. *The Lusiads* begins:

Arms and the heroes, from Lisbon's shore,
sailed through seas never dared before,
with awesome courage, forging their way
to the glorious kingdoms of the rising day.

The poem goes on to recite many events in Portuguese history, from the time of the Lusiads (the original pre-Roman natives) onward. Even today, Camões' words are quoted by modern Portuguese politicians in search of a heroic sound bite. And Portugal's national holiday, June 10, is known as Camões Day, remembering the day in 1580 when the great poet died. The stone monument here—with literary rather than maritime motifs—is an empty tomb (his actual burial spot is unknown).

• *Now head up to the front of the church, and the...*

❺ Renaissance Altar: Nearly everything here survived the 1755 earthquake, except for the stained glass (the replacement glass is from 1940). In the niches surrounding the main altar, elephants—a Far Eastern symbol of power, more powerful and kingly than the lion—support two kings and two queens (King Manuel I is front-left). Many Portuguese churches (such as the cathedrals in downtown Lisbon and Évora) were renovated in Renaissance and Baroque times, resulting in an odd mix of dark, older naves and pretty pastel altars.

Skip the **sacristy** (entrance in the corner), a single-columned room wrapped in paintings on wood featuring scenes from the life of St. Jerome (not worth the admission fee). Instead, do an about-face and head up the aisle on the right, back toward the entrance (noticing more elephants in the transept). You'll pass **seven wooden confessional doors** (on your right). Notice the ornamental carving around the second one: a festival of faces from newly discovered corners of the world. Head back toward the entry.

• *Under a ceiling that's a veritable* Boy Scout's Handbook *of rope and knots is the...*

❻ Tomb of Vasco da Gama: On the night of July 7, 1497, in the small chapel that once stood here, da Gama (1460-1524) prayed for a safe voyage. The next day, he set sail from Belém with four ships (see the caravel carved in the middle of the tomb's side) and 150 men. He was armed with state-of-the-art maps and sailing technology, such as the carved armillary sphere (to the right of the caravel)—a globe surrounded by movable rings designed to deter-  mine the positions of the sun or other stars to help sailors track their location on earth. (Some say its diagonal slash is symbolic of the unwritten pact and ambition of Spain and Portugal to split the world evenly, but it actually represents the path of the planets as they move across the heavens.)

Da Gama's mission? To confirm what earlier navigators had hypothesized—that the ocean recently discovered when Bartolomeu Dias rounded Africa's Cape of Good Hope was the same one seen by overland travelers to India. Hopefully, da Gama would find a direct sea route to the vast, untapped wealth of Asia. The symbols on the tomb show the icons of the period—the cross (symbolizing the religious military order of the soldier-monks who funded these voyages), the caravel (representing the method of travel), and Portugal's trading power around the globe (the result).

By Christmas, da Gama rounded the Cape of Good Hope. After battling hostile Arabs in Mozambique, he hired an Arab guide to pilot the ships to India, arriving on the southwest coast in Calicut (from which we get the word "calico") in May 1498. He traded for spices, networked with the locals for future outposts, battled belligerent chiefs, and then headed back home. Da Gama and his crew arrived home to Lisbon in September 1499 (after two years and two months on the seas) and were greeted with all-out Vasco-mania. The few spices he'd returned with (many were lost in transit) were worth a staggering fortune. Portugal's Golden Age was launched.

King Manuel dubbed da Gama "Admiral of the Sea of India" and sent him out again, this time to subdue the Indian people, establish more trade outposts, and again return home to wealth and honor. Da Gama died on Christmas Eve 1524, in India. His memory lives on due to the tribute of two men: Manuel, who built this large church, and Luís de Camões (honored opposite Vasco), who turned da Gama's history-making voyage into an epic poem.

• *Leave the church, turn right, purchase your ticket, pick up the included audioguide, and enter the...*

❼ **Cloister:** This restored cloister is the architectural highlight of Belém. The lacy arcade is Manueline; the simpler diamond and decorative rose frieze above the top floor is Renaissance. Study

Manueline Architecture, c. 1480-1580

Portugal's unique decorative style (from its peak of power under King Manuel I, the Fortunate, r. 1495-1521) reflects the wealth of the times and the many cultural influences of the Age of Discovery. It is more an ornamental than structural style, blending late Gothic features with Mudejar (Moorish) elements. Craftsmen applied it equally to buildings with pointed Gothic or rounded Renaissance arches; you'll see elaborate Manueline carved stonework particularly around windows and doors.

The Manueline aesthetic is ornate, elaborate, and intertwined, often featuring symbols from a family's coat of arms (shields with castles, crosses, lions, banners, and crowns) or motifs from the sea (rope-like columns or borders, knots, shells, coral, anchors, and nets). Manuel's personal symbol was the armillary sphere—a celestial globe—which was an indispensable navigational aid for sailors. You'll also see imports of the age, from opium poppies to exotic animals.

Architecture students will recognize elements from Gothic's elaborate tracery, the abstract designs of Moorish culture, similarities to Spain's intricate Plateresque style (which dates from the same time), and the elongated excesses of Italian Mannerism.

the carvings, especially the gargoyles above the lower set of arches. Among these functioning rainspouts, find a monkey, a kitten, and a cricket.

Heads of state are often received in the cloister with a warm welcome. This is also the site of many important treaty signings, such as Portugal's admittance to the European Union in 1986. Turn left and do a clockwise spin around this fine space.

In the first corner, a small lion-topped basin (where the monks washed up before meals) marks the entrance to the **refectory**, or dining hall—today an occasional concert venue— lined with fine 18th-century tiles. The tiles are considered textbook Rococo, which ignores the parameters set by the architecture (unlike Baroque, which works within the structure).

Halfway down the next stretch of cloister, on the left, is the burial spot of Portugal's most revered modern poet, **Fernando Pessoa** (see sidebar on page 50).

Continuing around, the former **chapter house** contains an exhibit of the lengthy restoration process, as well as the tomb of Alexandre Herculano, a Romantic 19th-century historian and poet. Quotes from Herculano adorn his tomb: "Sleep? Only the cold cadaver that doesn't feel sleeps. The soul flies and wraps itself around the feet of the All-Powerful."

• *Continuing around the cloister, find the stairs up.*

❸ **Upstairs:** At the top of the stairs, on the left, step into the Upper Choir (above the main door)—peering down into the vast sanctuary, at the feet of a powerful crucifix.

Back out in the upper cloister, circle around to find a bookshop (and the exit). All the way around are great cloister views. At the far end of the cloister is an exhibition that juxtaposes the historical timeline of this monastery and Portugal with contemporaneous world events (but no real artifacts).

▲Maritime Museum (Museu de Marinha)

If you're interested in Portugal's historic ships and navigational tools, this museum, which fills the west wing of the Monastery of Jerónimos (listed above), is worth a look. It's refreshingly uncrowded, and sailors love it.

Cost and Hours: €6.50, free first Sun of month, open daily 10:00-18:00, Oct-April until 17:00. It's at the far end of the long monastery building; facing the planetarium, the museum entrance is to your right, and its good **$$** cafeteria (open to the public) is to your left.

Visiting the Museum: You'll enter past huge statues of great explorers, then follow the one-way route (with English explanations) through the sprawling collection, offering a well-presented recap of an age when Portugal ruled the waves. And it's loaded with actual artifacts: nautical paintings, model ships, cannons, uniforms, and maps illustrating Portuguese explorations. The exhibit takes you right up to the present day, covering not just explorers and military vessels but also the fishing industry. You'll see the reconstructed king's and queen's staterooms from aboard King Carlos I's royal yacht *Amélia*. Then you'll walk outside (under a gallery) to reach a vast warehouse of actual boats—from rustic *rabelos* to yawls to ceremonial royal barges. The centerpiece is the massive barge of King João VI, with 38 oars pulled by some 80 oarsmen, and plush royal quarters at the stern.

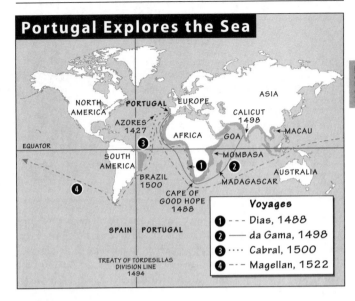

Portugal Explores the Sea

Voyages
- ❶ --- Dias, 1488
- ❷ —— da Gama, 1498
- ❸ ···· Cabral, 1500
- ❹ --- Magellan, 1522

LISBON

▲Monument to the Discoveries (Padrão dos Descobrimentos)

In 1960, the city honored the 500th anniversary of the death of Prince Henry the Navigator by rebuilding this giant riverside

monument, which had originally been constructed for a 1940 world's fair. It takes the shape of a huge caravel ship, in full sail, with Henry at the helm and the great navigators, sailors, and explorers on board behind him. The elevator inside takes you up to the tip-top for a tingly vista—including a fine aerial view down over the mural in front.

Cost and Hours: €4; May-Sept daily 10:00-19:00; Oct-April Tue-Sun 10:00-18:00, closed Mon, tel. 213-031-950, www.padraodosdescobrimentos.pt.

Visiting the Monument: To get here, find the pedestrian tunnel under the busy boulevard, then walk around the huge monument. The 170-foot concrete structure shows that exploring the world was a team effort. The men who braved the unknown stand on the pointed, raised prow of a caravel, about to be launched into the Rio Tejo.

Leading the charge is Prince Henry the Navigator holding a model of a caravel and a map, followed by kneeling kings and soldiers who Christianized foreign lands with the sword. Behind

Caravels

These easily maneuverable trading ships were fast, small (80 feet), and light (100 tons), with few guns and three triangular-shaped sails (called lateen-rigged sails) that could pivot quickly to catch the wind. They were ideal for sailing along coastlines. Many oceangoing caravels were also rigged with a square foresail for stability. (This photo shows the model held by Prince Henry on Belém's Monument to the Discoveries.) Columbus' *Niña* and *Pinta* were rerigged caravels.

Henry (on the west side, away from bridge), find the men who financed the voyages (King Manuel I, holding an armillary sphere, his personal symbol), those who glorified it in poems and paintings (like Luís de Camões, holding his famous poem *The Lusiads* on a scroll), and at the very end, the only woman, Philippa of Lancaster, Henry's British mother.

On the east side (closest to bridge—as you walk, notice the optical illusion of waves on the flat cobbled surface), Vasco da Gama stands with his eyes on the horizon and his hand on his sword. Magellan holds a circle, representing the round earth his ship circumnavigated, while in front of him, Pedro Cabral puts his hand to his heart, thankful to have (perhaps accidentally) discovered Brazil. Various monks, navigators with maps, and crusaders with flags complete the crew. Check out the pillory, decorated with the Portuguese coat of arms and a cross, erected in each place discovered by the Portuguese—leaving no doubt as to who was in charge.

In the **marble map in the pavement** (a gift from South Africa) in front of the Monument to the Discoveries, follow Portugal's explorers as they inched out into monster-infested waters at the edge of the world. From their tiny, isolated nation in Europe, the Portuguese first headed south to the coast of Morocco, conquering the Muslims of Ceuta in God's name (1415), and gaining strategic control of the mouth of the Mediterranean. They braved the open Atlantic to the west and southwest, stumbling on the Madeiras (1420), which Prince Henry planted with vineyards, and the remote Azore Islands (Açores, 1427).

Meanwhile, the Portuguese slowly moved southward, hugging the African coast, each voyage building on the knowledge from previous expeditions. They cleared the biggest psychological hump when Gil Eanes sailed around Cape Bojador (western Sahara, 1434)—the border of the known world—and into the equatorial seas where it was thought that sea monsters lurked, no winds blew, and ships would be incinerated in the hot sun. Eanes survived, re-

The Age of Discovery, 1400-1600

In 1560, you could sail from Lisbon to China without ever losing sight of land explored by Portugal. The riches of the world poured into the tiny nation—spices from India and Java (black pepper, cinnamon); ivory, diamonds, and slaves (sold to New World plantations) from Africa; sugarcane, gold, and diamonds from Brazil; and, from everywhere, knowledge of new plants, animals, and customs. How did tiny Portugal pull this off?

First, its people were motivated by greed, hoping to break the Arab and Venetian monopoly on Eastern luxury goods (the price of pepper was jacked up 1,000 percent by the time it reached European dinner tables). They were also driven by a crusading Christian spirit, a love of science, and a spirit of adventure. An entire 15th-century generation was obsessed with finding the legendary kingdom of the fabulously wealthy Christian named "Prester John," supposedly located in either India or Africa. (The legend may be based on a historical figure from around 1120 who visited the pope in Rome as "patriarch of India.")

Portugal also had certain natural advantages. Its Atlantic location led to a strong maritime tradition. A unified nation-state (one of Europe's first) financed and coordinated expeditions. And a core of technology-savvy men used and developed their expansive knowledge of navigational devices, astronomy, maps, shipbuilding, and languages.

turning home with 200 Africans in chains, the first of what would become a lucrative, abhorrent commodity. Two generations later, Bartolomeu Dias rounded the southern tip of Africa (Cabo da Boa Esperança, 1488), discovering the sea route to Asia that Vasco da Gama (1498) and others would exploit to colonize India, Indonesia, Japan, and China (Macao in 1557, on the south coast).

In 1500, Pedro Cabral (along with Dias and 1,200 men) took a wi-i-i-ide right turn on the way down the African coast, hoping to avoid windless seas, and landed on the tip of Brazil. The country proved to be an agricultural goldmine for Portugal, which profited from sugar plantations worked by African slaves. Two hundred years later, gold and gemstones were discovered in Brazil, jump-starting the Portuguese economy again.

In 1520, Portuguese Ferdinand Magellan, employed by Spain, sailed west with five ships and 270 men, broke for R&R in Rio, continued through the Straits of Magellan (tip of South America), and suffered through mutinies, scurvy, and dinners of sawdust and ship rats before touching land in Guam. Magellan was killed in battle in the Philippines, but one remaining ship continued west and arrived back in Europe, having circumnavigated the globe after 30 months at sea.

By 1560, Portugal's global empire had peaked. Tiny-but-filthy-rich Portugal claimed (though they didn't actually occupy) the entire coastline of Africa, Arabia, India, the Philippines, and south China—a continuous stretch from Lisbon to Macao—plus Brazil. The Treaty of Tordesillas (1494) with Spain divvied up the colonial world between the two nations, split at 45 degrees west longitude (bisecting South America—and explaining why Brazil speaks Portuguese and the rest of the continent speaks Spanish) and 135 degrees east longitude (bisecting the Philippines and Australia).

But all that wealth was wasted on Portugal's ruling class, who neglected to reinvest it in the future. Easy money ruined the traditional economy and stunted industry, hurting the poor. Over the next four centuries, one by one, Portugal's colonies were lost to other European nations or to local revolutions. Today, only the (largely autonomous) islands of the Azores and Madeiras remain from the once-global empire.

▲Belém Tower (Torre de Belém)

Perhaps the purest Manueline building in Portugal (built 1515-1520), this white tower protected Lisbon's harbor. Today it symbolizes the voyages that made Lisbon powerful, with carved stone representing ropes, Manuel's coat of arms, armillary spheres, and shields with the cross of the Order of Christ, charged with spreading the faith in new territories.

Cost and Hours: €6, €12 combo-ticket with Monastery of Jerónimos, free first Sun of month, Tue-Sun 10:00-18:30, Oct-April until 17:30, closed Mon; from the monument it's a pretty, 10-minute waterfront walk, but be ready to detour around the big yacht marina; tel. 213-620-034, www.torrebelem.pt.

Visiting the Tower: This was the last sight sailors saw as they left their homeland, and the first as they returned, loaded with gold, spices, and social diseases. When the tower was built, the river went nearly to the walls of the monastery, and the tower was midriver. Its interior is pretty bare, but the views of the bridge, river, and Cristo Rei statue are worth the 120 steps.

The floatplane on the grassy lawn is a monument to the first flight across the South Atlantic (Portugal to Brazil) in 1922. The original plane (which beat Charles Lindbergh's *Spirit of Saint Louis* across the North Atlantic by five years) is in Belém's Maritime Museum.

If you're choosing between towers, the Monument to the Discoveries is probably the better choice, because it offers a better view of the monastery. Both towers are interesting to see from the outside, whether or not you go up.

Ferry from Belém to Porto Brandão

For a delightfully untouristy little adventure, consider having lunch across the river in **Porto Brandão.** The ferry terminal is immediately in front of the National Coach Museum, across a busy road and train tracks (€1.65 each way—or €1.15 zapping with Viva Viagem card, 8-minute cruise, ferries depart on the hour and half hour except hourly from 13:30-15:30, last ferry departs 23:00 weekdays and 22:00 weekends; for a memorable Tejo experience, tall men can use the urinal while sticking their head out the porthole). Boats continue to Trafaria before returning to Belém via Porto Brandão. Upon arrival, carefully confirm return times.

Porto Brandão is a tiny (and dead) three-street town whose harborfront square has several good fish restaurants. I like cozy, blue-and-white-tiled **$$$ Restaurante Porto Brandão.** Their *bacalhau à lagareiro* is for garlic lovers. The *cataplana* (a traditional fish-and-veggie stew) and seafood fondue meals are made for two but stuff three (daily 12:00-15:00 & 18:00-23:00, Rua Bento Jesus Caraça 25, tel. 212-959-145).

MODERN LISBON

Lisbon celebrated the 500th anniversary of Vasco da Gama's voyage to India by hosting Expo '98 here at Parque das Nações. The theme was "The Ocean and the Seas," emphasizing the global importance of healthy, clean waters. And today, the city has thoughtfully repurposed the fairgrounds into a park and shopping mall. To get out of the quaint, Pombal-esque old town and enjoy a peek at some modern architecture, ride the Metro to Oriente station. From here, you can stroll through an airy shopping mall, explore the sprawling site of the 1998 world's fair, and promenade with locals along the Rio Tejo riverfront park. It's worth a visit any day, but makes sense on Monday (when most museums in town are closed). It's also particularly vibrant when people are out early on summer evenings and weekends.

• *Your visit begins when you step off the train, inside...*

Oriente Train Station (Gare do Oriente)

Oriente means "facing east." This impressive hub ties together trains (to the Algarve and Évora), the Metro, and buses under a swooping concrete roof designed by the Spanish architect Santiago Calatrava.

• *Facing Oriente station across the street is...*

Vasco da Gama Mall

The inviting, soaring glass facade of Lisbon's top shopping mall—originally the grand entrance to Expo '98—was also designed by Calatrava (daily 9:00-24:00). Stepping into the mall, you'll see that its design seems to have been inspired by the main hall of a luxury cruise ship. Notice the water cascading down the glass roof—a clever and eye-pleasing way to keep things cool and avoid any greenhouse effect. From the mall's entrance, climb the stairs to a small outdoor terrace for a good view back at the train station. Look up at the two skyscraping luxury condo buildings. With fine transportation connections and modern office space, this area holds lots of promise, both for residences and businesses. Microsoft set up its Portuguese headquarters here, and the Portuguese national court occupies contemporary new buildings nearby.

Now stroll through the upper level of the mall to the opposite end, where you can step out to another outdoor terrace. From here you can look toward the river and survey Parque das Nações—the grounds for Expo '98. Straight ahead are the flags lining the Grand Esplanade (described next). The striped oval dome to the left, once the Atlantic Pavilion (Pavilhão Atlântico), is now an 18,000-seat concert hall. The oil refinery tower far to the right marks the west end of the park and is a remnant of the industrial wasteland that was here before the fair.

• *Exiting the mall at the far end from the train station, you'll be smack-dab in the middle of...*

▲▲Parque das Nações

From the Vasco de Gama Mall, you're at the top of the Grand Esplanade (Rossio Olivais), lined by 155 flags—one for each coun-

try represented at Expo '98. The flags are arranged in alphabetical order, so the first ones are South Africa (Africa dul Sul), Albania, and Germany (Alemanha). In the middle you'll find the US (Estados Unidos), Spain (Espanha), and Estonia side by side.

At the far end of the line of flags you'll reach a basin (on your right) that predates the fair.

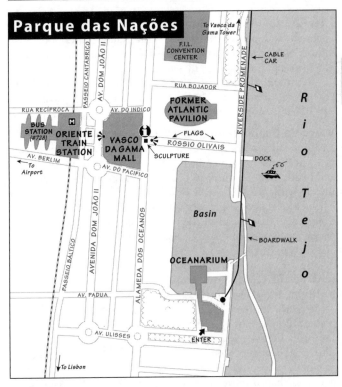

Back before World War II, this was a watery "parking lot" (just 1.5 yards deep) for seaplanes. Across the basin to your right, the blocky building that resembles an aircraft carrier with a spiky rooftop is the Lisbon Oceanarium (described next)—the big hit of the fair and still the park's major attraction. From behind that the cable car (€4 one-way, €6 round-trip, nothing special, daily 11:00-19:00) drifts east to the Vasco da Gama Tower, which marks that end of the park. Two miles away, built as part of the 1998 celebrations, is the Vasco da Gama Bridge. A delightful promenade (Caminho dos Pinheiros; "The Way of the Pine Trees") runs along the riverfront from the marina all the way to a park at the base of the Vasco de Gama Bridge.

Lisbon Oceanarium (Oceanário de Lisboa)

Europe's largest aquarium—housed in what looks like a drilling platform or a big, modern ship at sea—simulates four different oceanic underwater and shoreline environments, from the Atlantic to the Pacific to the Indian to the Arctic. You'll circle around the upper level, seeing surface dwellers from each climate (such as otters, puffins, penguins, and other sea birds). Then you'll head downstairs and do another loop, this time seeing underwater creatures. The centerpiece—which you'll keep circling back to—is an enormous and mesmerizing central tank crammed full of fascinating fish big and small, including several sharks. Weekday-morning school groups are also happily on display.

Cost and Hours: €14, €9 for kids 4-12, daily 10:00-20:00, Nov-March until 19:00, last entry one hour before closing, tel. 218-917-000, www.oceanario.pt.

Vasco da Gama Bridge (Ponte Vasco da Gama)

Europe's longest bridge (10.7 miles) was opened in 1998 to connect the Expo '98 grounds with the south side of the Rio Tejo, and to alleviate the traffic jams on Lisbon's only other bridge over the river, the 25th of April Bridge. The Vasco de Gama Bridge helped connect north and south Portugal, back when a freeway was a big deal in this late-to-develop European nation. Built low to the water, the bridge's towers and cables are meant to suggest the sails of a caravel ship.

EAST LISBON

National Tile Museum (Museu Nacional do Azulejo)

Filling the Convento da Madre de Deus, the museum features piles of tiles, which, as you've probably noticed, are an art form in Portugal. They've tried to show-case the tiles as they would have originally appeared (note the diamond-shaped staircase tiles), but the presentation is low-tech, and the posted English explanations are dry. You can see more exciting tiles in situ throughout Portugal. But for aficionados this is a handy one-stop survey.

And the circa-1700 tile panorama of Lisbon (upstairs) is fascinating, letting you pick out landmarks that were toppled in the 1755 quake.

Cost and Hours: €5, free first Sun of month; open Tue-Sun 10:00-18:00, closed Mon; located about a mile east of Praça do Comércio—15 minutes on bus #794 from Praça do Comércio or bus #742 from near the Gulbenkian Museum (bus leaves around the corner from São Sebastião Metro station—along Rua Marquês de Fronteira), both buses stop right at museum entrance on Rua da Madre de Deus 4, tel. 218-100-340, mnazulejo.im-ip.pt.

Azulejos

During visits to neighboring Spain, King Manuel I not only acquired wives, but he also obtained several thousand tiles to decorate palaces throughout Portugal. Vibrant colors must have attracted the king's attention, and some examples from his visits can still be seen in the National Palace in Sintra. It wasn't long before Portuguese artists began producing them for local clients, and the tiles—called *azulejos* (ah-zoo-LAY-zhoos, from an Arab word meaning "small polished stone")—became synonymous with the seafaring empire.

The biggest challenge for early artisans was keeping colors from running together during firing. A number of techniques developed to solve this problem: *Alicatados* are mosaic pieces, cut after firing, to form intricate geometric patterns; *corda seca* fills thick outlines of manganese oxide with different colors, like a children's coloring book; and *aresta* sculpts color wells directly into the tile. The biggest breakthrough came with the development of *majólica*, or *faiança*—the undecorated clay tile is baked first, then covered with an opaque glaze that makes a canvas for the painted design, which is set by a second firing.

Brazilians loved tilework, too, and after the return of the Portuguese king to European shores, factories began producing tilework for the masses. But tilework began to fall out of fashion by the early 20th century. Then Lisbon's 1959 Metro system gave tile artists a new playground. While not originally in the budget, artist Maria Keil could not bear to see the walls vacant. Her original designs are still on display, and future artists continue to make the Metro an underground art museum.

Unfortunately, others have noticed the beauty (and profitability) of historic tilework panels. Theft is common—often for resale on the black market—and many of Lisbon's older panels are at risk. In the past decade, local watch groups have documented several hundred cases of missing panels and helped recover several of them. Think twice before purchasing tilework at the Feira da Ladra flea market.

To go on your own *azulejo* scavenger hunt, check out Endless Mile's tile guide to Lisbon that lists nearly 100 of the city's best tile panels (www.endlessmile.com).

SOUTH OF LISBON, ACROSS THE RIVER
▲25th of April Bridge (Ponte 25 de Abril)

Imagine that before 1966, there was no way across the Rio Tejo except by ferry. This suspension bridge—1.5 miles long (3,280 feet

between the towers—bears an uncanny resemblance to San Francisco's Golden Gate Bridge (it was built in 1966 by the same company that made its famous cousin—but notice the lower deck for train tracks). The foundations are sunk 260 feet below the surface into the riverbed, making it the world's deepest bridge. Originally named for the dictator Salazar, the bridge was renamed for the date of Portugal's 1974 revolution and liberation. For a generation, natives would show their political colors by choosing which name to use. While conservative Portuguese called it the "Salazar Bridge," liberals referred to it as the "25th of April Bridge" (just as Washington, D.C.'s airport is still called "National" by some and "Reagan" by others).

Cristo Rei Statue (Christ the King)

A huge, 330-foot concrete statue of Christ (à la Rio de Janeiro, in the former Portuguese colony of Brazil) overlooks Lisbon from across the Rio Tejo, stretching its arms wide to

symbolically bless the city (or, as less reverent Portuguese say, "to dive into the river"). Lisbon's cardinal, inspired by a visit to Rio de Janeiro in 1936, wanted a replica built back home. Increased support came after an appeal was made to Our Lady of Fátima in 1940 to keep Portugal out of World War II. Portugal survived the war relatively unscathed, and funds were collected to build this statue in appreciation. After 10 years of construction, it opened to the public in 1959. It's now a sanctuary and pilgrimage site, and the chapel inside holds regular Sunday Mass. The statue was designed to be seen from a distance, and there's little reason to go to the trouble of actually visiting it. If you do visit, an elevator will take you to the top for a panoramic view: From left to right, see Belém, the 25th of April Bridge, downtown Lisbon (Praça do Comércio and the green Alfama hilltop with the castle), and the long Vasco da Gama Bridge.

Cost and Hours: €5, daily 9:30-18:15, slightly later in summer, tel. 212-751-000, www.cristorei.pt.

Getting There: To get to Cristo Rei, catch the 10-minute ferry from downtown Lisbon to Cacilhas (4/hour, see

"Public Ferry Ride to Cacilhas" on page 19), then hop on the bus marked *101 Cristo Rei* (3/hour, exit ferry dock left into the maze of bus stops to find the #20 stop with the "101 Cristo Rei" schedule under the awning, 15-minute ride). Because of bridge tolls to enter Lisbon, taxis from the site are expensive. Consider taking a late-morning ferry-and-bus connection to Cristo Rei; catch a taxi from the statue to Porto Brandão and have lunch there (see page 79); and ferry direct to Belém and see the sights. For drivers, the most efficient visit is a quick stop on your way to or from Évora or the Algarve.

WEST OF LISBON, ON THE COAST
Cascais

The seafront resort town of Cascais (kahsh-KAYSH), about 17 miles due west of Lisbon, provides a fun and quick escape from

the big city of Lisbon. Before the rise of the Algarve, Cascais was the haunt of Portugal's rich and beautiful. Today it's an elegant and inviting escape from the city with pleasant beaches and a relaxing ambience (see map on page 127).

Before the 20th century, aristocrats wanted to avoid the sun and exaggerate their lily-white skin—and a day at the beach made just no sense. But about 1900, the Portuguese queen Maria Pia (daughter of King Victor Emmanuel II of Italy) made Cascais her summer vacation getaway—and Portugal's high society followed. A train line made Cascais easily accessible from the city, and between the world wars, the area was developed as a kind of Portuguese answer to the French Riviera.

Getting There: Just hop the train at Lisbon's Cais do Sodré station (M: Cais do Sodré) and you're in Cascais in 40 minutes or less (3/hour, www.cp.pt).

Visiting Cascais: The Cascais station (the last stop on the Cais do Sodré line) faces the town center. From there, the main cobbled street, Rua Frederico Arouca, parallels the waterfront past shops and eateries to Largo Cidade Vitória, where you'll find a helpful TI kiosk (daily 9:00-18:00).

Cascais still has a fishing industry. Adjacent to the TI, you'll find the Serviços de Pescado, a wholesale fish market where most days at 17:00 visitors can witness the quick fish auction as local retailers snap up the day's catch. Just beyond is the main beach and a palm-lined promenade leading to an old fort. Deeper into town are several little museums; the Museu do Maris is best for the story of the town and its relationship with the sea (free, Tue-Sun 10:00-17:00, closed Mon, about 10 minutes from the center at Rua Júlio Pereira de Mello, www.cm-cascais.pt/museumar).

Returning to Lisbon via Estoril: A paved seaside promenade leads from Cascais past several beaches to **Estoril,** its sister beach resort town (a half-hour stroll away). Of the several small sandy beaches, Praia da Conceição and Praia das Moitas conveniently have showers. If you have time and like seaside strolls, I'd recommend walking this strip and catching the train back to Lisbon from Estoril (all trains stop at both Estoril and Cascais).

Estoril is famous for its casino and many grand hotels. From the Lisbon-Cascais train you can look past the Estoril station and across the park at the modern casino. Ian Fleming hatched his first 007 story here in the early days of World War II, when Portugal was neutral and this area was a hotbed of spies. The Estoril casino where Fleming gambled must have been part of the inspiration for his first James Bond novel, *Casino Royale.* But Cascais rather than Estoril is clearly the most rewarding stop for today's traveler.

Shopping in Lisbon

Lisbon is a marvelous shopping city: creative, with a trendy vibe but also respectful of tradition—and it's cheap. My suggestions below focus on one-off shops that specialize in unique slices of Lisbon life. I've also included a few big malls for handy one-stop shopping.

SOUVENIR IDEAS

The shops mentioned here are scattered around central Lisbon, but most are concentrated in the hip and artsy Chiado district.

Cork

Portugal is famous for its cork, a versatile material that can be put to hundreds of uses. Shops all over town show off practical and eye-pleasing items made of cork, from handbags to wallets to umbrellas. For fashionable, top-end products, head up to the flagship store of the internationally respected **Pelcor,** in the Príncipe Real shopping zone (closed Sun, Pátio do Tijolo 4, just off Rua Dom Pedro V, www.pelcor.pt). In the Bairro Alto, **Cork & Co** is a more affordable little boutique with a wider array of products—including jewelry (closed Sun, Rua das Salgadeiras 6-10, www.corkandcompany.pt).

Wine

If you're in the market to buy some fine bottles of wine to enjoy in Portugal or to ship home, two handy options sit near each other just below the cathedral. While touristy—and with somewhat inflated prices—both have helpful staff who can talk you through your options and arrange shipping. (They may suggest that you make your selection in the shop, then place your order on their website.) **Napoleão Wine Shop** has free samples of three unique Portuguese options: port, *vinho verde*, and *ginjinha* (daily, main branch at Rua Conceição 16 specializes in Portuguese wines, second branch across the street also has international booze; www.napoleao.eu). **Garrafeira Nacional** has a similar set-up in the Baixa (closed Sun, Rua da Conceição 20/26) and a user-friendly location inside Mercado da Ribeira (www.garrafeiranacional.com).

Azulejos (Colored Tiles)

Portugal's iconic colored tiles make vivid souvenirs—for use as trivets, wall hangings, or even (for the ambitious) a backsplash renovation project. It's easy to find affordable, basic, painted replicas of classic *azulejo* designs—many souvenir shops stock a small selection. For better-quality replica *azulejos*, try **Viúva Lamego** (closed Sat-Sun, in the trendy Intendente neighborhood at Largo do Intendente 25; for more on Intendente, see page 93), **Fábrica Sant'Anna** (closed Sun, in the Chiado at Rua do Alecrim 95), or the more tourist-oriented **Loja dos Descobrimentos** (daily, below the cathedral at Rua dos Bacalhoeiros 12). If you're shopping for authentic antique tiles, try **d'Orey Azulejos** (closed Sun, in the Chiado at Rua do Alecrim 68) or the cramped **Antiquário Solar** (a.k.a. Albuquerque e Sousa; closed Sat afternoon and all day Sun, in the Bairro Alto at Rua Dom Pedro V 68-70).

Conservas (Canned Fish)

Canned fish (collectively called *conservas*) is a Portuguese staple, are not the harsh, cured-in-salt sardines you might think of back home. This is quality fish in olive oil (sardines, cod, mackerel, and tuna are most common), often mixed with herbs, spices, or infused oils to impart extra flavor. Best of all, colorful packaging turns the cans into great souvenirs or gifts, and makes window-shopping a delight. The best *conservas* place in town—near Mercado da Ribeira—is **Loja Das Conservas,** with shelves upon shelves of attractively decorated cans from all over Portugal. This shop is operated by a local consortium, and prides itself on educating its customers (daily, Rua do Arsenal 130). In the upper part of the Alfama, just below the castle, **Miss Can** sells a small selection of their own production, with clever packaging and a little café where you can enjoy a light meal (see "Eating in Lisbon," daily, Largo do Contador Mor 19). And in the Chiado, you'll find the upscale **Conserveira da Trinidade,** with a carefully curated selection and the option to nibble right there (daily, Rua Nova da Trinidade 11).

LISBON

To Praça Marquês de Pombal, Gulbenkian Museum & 23

To Príncipe Real Garden, Shopping, 9 1 & 18

RUA ST. GLORIA

R. DOM PEDRO V

R. DA ROSA

ELEVADOR DA GLÓRIA

São Pedro de Alcântara Park

R. COELHO

T.S. PEDRO

S. P. ALCÂNTARA

R. N. MOUROS

AVENIDA DA LIBERDADE

RUA DA GLÓRIA

OBELISK

Praça dos Restauradores

Restauradores

ABEP TICKET KIOSK

NAT'L THEATER

To Elevador do Lavra

COLISEU

CONDES SAO JOSÉ

S. ANT. PORTAS SANTAO

REGEDOR

C. DE SANTANA

CALÇADA NOVA

R.M. VAZ

R. BARCO D.GRAÇA

Largo de São Domingos

SÃO DOMINGOS

R. QUEIRÓS

R. DOM DUARTE

ROSSIO

RUA DE SANTA JUSTA

RUA DOS SAPATEIROS

ROSSIO TRAIN STATION

IGREJA SÃO ROQUE

MUSEU DE ARTE SACRA

Largo do Cadoval

Rossio (Praça Dom Pedro IV)

Rossio

B Bus Tours

Praça da Figueira

#12E & 15E

PORRATEM

RUA DA ROSA

RUA DA ATALAIA

RUA LUIZ SORIANO

R. S. BEN.

TR. BOA HORA

TR. AGUA FLOR

R. DO GREMIO

TR. QUEIMADA

Largo Trinidade Coelho

R. C. DUQUE

R. DO DUQUE

T. DEZEMBRO

R. CONDESA

ARCH BESTEGA

BAIRRO ALTO

12

TEATRO DA TRINDADE

17

CONVENTO DO CARMO

ELEVADOR STA. JUSTA

BAIXA

TR. DOS FIEIS DE DEUS

T. MERCES

ROSA DA

RUA DO NORTE

R. GAVEA

R. ESPERA

RUA NOVA TRINDADE

RUA DA TRINDADE

R. DA OLIVEIRA

R. DO CARMO

16

Largo do Carmo

RUA DA ASSUNÇÃO

R. D. CORREEIROS

RUA DA PRATA

R. BARROCA

2

CHIADO

RUA GARRETT

ARMAZENS DO CHIADO MALL

Baixa-Chiado

21

RUA AUREA

RUA VITORIA

RUA AUGUSTA

R. CAL. R. LORETO

Praça de Camões

#28E

#28E

ELEVADOR DA BICA

R. H. SECA

R. DA MENDA

Largo Barão Quintela

8

M Baixa-Chiado

15

SERPA PINTO

13

R. CAPELO

R. S. FRAN.

RUA IVENS

RUA DO CRUCEIRO

RUA DO OURO

RUA DE

BICA

R. ST. CAT.

T. G.

COUSSUL

6

FLORES

RUA DO ALECRIM

RUA A. MARIA CARDOSO

RUA D. BRAGANÇA

SÃO CARLOS THEATER

BIBLIOTECA PUBLICA

Largo da Publica

C. S. FRANCISCO

#28E

RUA DE SÃO JULIÃO

ARCH

"PINK STREET" (NIGHTLIFE)

R. ATAIDE

RUA S. PAULO

RUA NOVA DO CARVALHO

R. RIBEIRA NOVA

4

13 19

MERCADO DA RIBEIRA

RUA VITOR CORDON

#28E

Praça do Municipio

10

RUA DO ARSENAL

RUA DO COMÉRCIO

LISBON WALKER

JOSÉ I STATUE

i

#794 & Aerobus #1

14

Praça Duque de Terceira

#15E

Cais do Sodré

To Belém

CAIS DO SODRÉ TRAIN STATION

Trains to Belém, Estoril & Cascais

AVE. DA RIBEIRA DAS NAUS

RIVER CRUISES

CAIS DO SODRÉ FERRY TERMINAL

To Cacilhas

❶	To Pelcor
❷	Cork & Co.
❸	Napoleão Wine Shop
❹	Garrafeira Nacional (2)
❺	To Viúva Lamego
❻	Fábrica Sant'Anna
❼	Loja dos Descobrimentos
❽	d'Orey Azulejos

LISBON

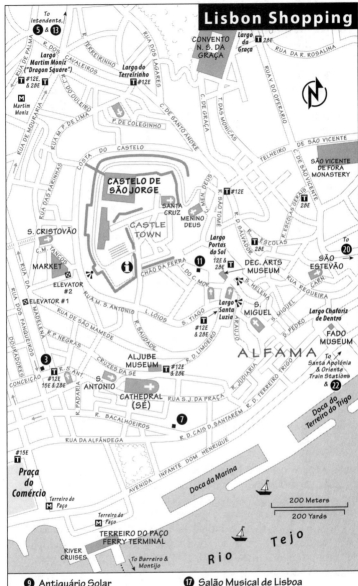

Lisbon Shopping

- **9** Antiquário Solar
- **10** Loja Das Conservas
- **11** Miss Can
- **12** Conserveira da Trinidade
- **13** A Vida Portuguesa (3)
- **14** Lisbon Shop (2)
- **15** Loja da Burel
- **16** Luvaria Ulisses
- **17** Salão Musical de Lisboa
- **18** To Príncipe Real Shopping District
- **19** Mercado da Ribeira
- **20** To Feira da Ladra Flea Market
- **21** Armazéns do Chiado Mall
- **22** To Vasco da Gama Mall
- **23** To El Corte Inglés

Other Quality Portuguese Souvenirs

A Vida Portuguesa is the best shop in town for a well-chosen selection of high-quality, artisanal Portuguese products—everything from stationery and toiletries to housewares and decorative objects to toys and jewelry (daily, Rua Anchieta 11, www.avidaportuguesa. com). They have two other locations: a bigger flagship store in the Intendente neighborhood (daily, Largo do Intendente 23), and a smaller location inside the Mercado do Ribeira.

If you're in a pinch for souvenirs, local TIs have a small but nicely stocked **"Lisbon Shop"** with some basic items emblazoned with Lisbon's trademarks—sardines, fado, or trolleys—as well as fado CDs, at prices typically better than elsewhere in the Baixa (daily, main branch in Praça do Comércio TI, smaller selection at the TI on Praça das Restauradores).

Woolens: The delightful **Loja da Burel** boutique showcases fashionable items made from the heavy Portuguese wool called *burel*. This company took over an abandoned wool factory high in the mountains and brought back skilled but out-of-work old-timers to revive a dormant industry. Today the factory churns out high-quality blankets, handbags, coats, shoes, and other products with a mix of traditional and contemporary style (daily, Rua Serpa Pinto 15B, www.burelfactory.com).

Leather Gloves: The Lisbon institution **Luvaria Ulisses** sells top-quality leather gloves *(luvas)* one pair at a time, with individual attention to help you find just the right style and fit. The shop is nestled into a tiny storefront just a few steps off Rossio. You squeeze into the shop, then the clerks squeeze your hands into the gloves: they'll nest your elbow on a dainty little pillow, squirt a puff of talcum powder into the glove, then massage your fingers in, one at a time (after a visit here, you'll suddenly appreciate the expression "fits like a glove"). While popular with tourists from faraway lands (expect to wait at busy times), they're still cranking out quality gloves at decent prices (many pairs around €50-60, closed Sun, Rua do Carmo 87, www.luvariaulisses.com).

Musical Instruments: If you're captivated by fado and want to check out a Portuguese guitar, **Salão Musical de Lisboa** has a fine selection and a handy location, right on the charming Campo de Carmo square (closed Sun, Rua da Oliveira ao Carmo 2, www. salaomusical.com).

SHOPPING ZONES

For a focused shopping spree, consider one of these areas. Intendente, described in "Entertainment in Lisbon," also has a few fun shops.

Príncipe Real Shopping District

For cutting-edge fashion and design, and one of Lisbon's most appealing little green parks, head to the Príncipe Real Garden at the top of the Chiado (about a five-minute walk or speedy bus trip from the top of the Elevador da Glória funicular).

The anchor of this area is the **Embaixada** complex, across the street from the park. Young entrepreneurs have taken over a grand 19th-century Arabian-style townhouse, given it a modern makeover, and filled its two floors with an array of high-end local designers and vendors that attract hipsters, well-dressed urbanites, and in-the-know tourists. You'll see fashion, home decor, kidswear, high-end tailors,  art galleries, pop-up shops, and much more. Climb the grand old staircase, on scuffed tiles and under peeling plaster ceilings, to feel the artful "ramshackle chic" vibe. In the atrium, the Less café has affordable light meals and a gin bar; there's also a little garden café out back (daily 12:00-20:00, Praça do Príncipe Real 26).

Just a few doors down (walking with the park on your left), at the smaller but similarly chic **REAL "Slow Retail" Concept Store,** creative local vendors display their wares in a clean, cool, industrial-mod, space. You'll see stacks of coffee-table books, creative housewares, summer dresses, burlap backpacks, colorful shoes and sandals, hipster toddler garb, and horn-rimmed sunglasses (Mon-Wed 10:30-20:00, Thu-Sat until 23:00, closed Sun, Praça do Príncipe Real 20).

A bit farther down are more fun shops, including **Corallo,** where Bettina and Niccolò make their own chocolates and roast their own coffee (closed Sun, Rua da Escola Politécnica 4), and the old-school **Príncipe Real Enxovais,** specializing in top-quality linens for the home (daily, Rua da Escola Politécnica 12). And in the opposite direction, a block up Rua Dom Pedro V back toward the heart of the Chiado, is the **Pelcor** cork products flagship store (see earlier, under "Cork").

This is also a great part of town to get a bite; for details, see the Chiado listings in "Eating in Lisbon," later.

Mercado da Ribeira (a.k.a. Time Out Market)

This recently renovated market hall offers Lisbon's best one-stop shopping for culinary souvenirs (it's described in detail on page 112). In addition to bottles of wine, chocolates, canned fish, and other edible goodies, it has an outpost of Lisbon's best souvenir shop, A Vida Portuguesa. And, of course, it's also great for a meal. Most stalls are open daily from 12:00 to 24:00. Note that the Loja Das Conservas canned-fish shop is just down the street (see earlier, under "*Conservas*").

Flea Markets
On Tuesdays and Saturdays, the **Feira da Ladra flea market** attracts bargain hunters to Campo de Santa Clara in the Alfama (8:00-15:00, best in morning). A Sunday-morning **coin market** jingles at Mercado da Ribeira, listed above (9:00-13:00).

Shopping Malls and Department Stores
Lisbon has several malls and huge department stores (all open long hours daily). Most central is **Armazéns do Chiado,** with six modern floors—and handy elevators connecting the Baixa and the Chiado (food court on the sixth floor, www.armazensdochiado.com). North of downtown, **Vasco da Gama Mall** fills the grand entryway to the Expo '98 site at the Oriente train/Metro station (described on page 80). And the Spanish megadepartment store, **El Corte Inglés,** has a huge branch at the top of Edward VII Park (near Gulbenkian Museum at Avenida António Augusto de Aguiar 31, M: São Sebastião).

Entertainment in Lisbon

NIGHTLIFE
The Baixa is quiet at night, with a few touristy al fresco restaurants and not much else. Head instead up to the Bairro Alto for fado halls, bars, and the Miradouro de São Pedro de Alcântara (view terrace), a pleasant place to hang out. Nearby Rua Diario de Noticias is lined with busy bars and fun crowds spilling onto the street.

Rua Nova do Carvalho (a.k.a. Pink Street)
This happening, crazy street is a short walk downhill from the Chiado in the Cais do Sodré neighborhood (just behind Mercado da Ribeira). Rua Nova do Carvalho, otherwise known as "Pink Street," was once notorious as the sailors' red-light zone. Now the prostitutes are just painted onto the walls, and the made-over street is painted a bright pink. After the bars in other neighborhoods

close, late-night revelers hike 10 minutes from the Chiado down Rua do Alecrim to reach Pink Street. Surrounded by largely uninhabited Pombaline buildings, Pink Street's four bars are allowed to make noise—and they do—until very late into the night. Many of the nightspots here are rowdy, youthful dance halls with names like Tokyo, Musicbox, Viking, and Sabotage Rock Club, with a few striptease clubs mixed in. But the following places—lively earlier and accessible to a wider clientele—are my Pink Street picks.

Pensão Amor ("House of Love") is a velvety place for a cocktail. Wallpapered with sexy memories of the days when it was a brothel, it's a grungy tangle of corners to hang out in and enjoy a drink (or just stare at the graffiti), often against a backdrop of live jazz. It even has a sexy library if you feel like reading (no food, Rua Nova do Carvalho 38, also possible to enter from along the bridge at Rua do Alecrim 19, tel. 213-143-399).

Sol e Pesca Bar, a nostalgic reminder of the sailor-and-fisherman heritage of this street, sells drinks and preserved food in tins. Just browse the shelves of classic tinned seafood—from pâté and sardines to caviar—and wash down your salty seafood tapas with a glass of wine amid the lures and nets (Rua Nova do Carvalho 44, tel. 213-467-203).

Povo Lisboa is a trendy little bar serving delightful Portuguese tapas (from 18:00) and enlivening things with fado (from 20:00 weekdays or from 21:00 weekends, closed Mon, no cover—just buy a drink, light food, Rua Nova do Carvalho 32, tel. 213-473-403).

LxFactory

LxFactory is a typical riverside industrial zone gone shabby-chic. Passing through the factory gate (under the 25th of April Bridge), you'll find a youthful crowd sorting through a collection of restaurants, clubs, shops, and galleries. LxFactory is lively each night and all day on weekends (www.lxfactory.com).

Intendente

Intendente—just north of the Baixa—is emerging as a hip and happening zone, with a mellower energy (and fewer partying tourists) than the raucous Pink Street described earlier. This is where Lisbon's artsy hipsters gather to sip a drink, smoke a cigarette, and just hang out. Until recently a place locals avoided at night, today Intendente has impromptu cultural happenings and intriguing little bars and cafés. The epicenter is the main square, Largo do Intendente, which is tucked just off the main drag.

Getting There: Ride the Metro (M: Intendente) or walk 15 minutes up Rua de Palma from the top of Praça da Figueira. You'll pass through the entertaining Praça Martim Moniz, nicknamed "Dragon Square" (at M: Martim Moniz). This parklike neighborhood square comes with some basic world food stalls (including Brazilian) and a family-friendly vibe during the day.

Visiting Intendente: On the once-seedy Largo do Intendente—ringed with classic old buildings in various stages of deterioration and renovation—you'll find several cafés and shops. **Casa Independente,** a cultural venue with a chill and alternative vibe, has a nondescript entrance—but climb up the stairs to discover a ramshackle-chic bar and patio with light bites and cocktails (Tue-Sat 14:00-24:00, closed Sun-Mon, no sign, upstairs at Largo do Intendente 45, tel. 218-872-842, www.casaindependente.com). Other characteristic, pretentiously casual cafés have seating on the square, including the artsy **O das Jonas** (with light meals, closed Tue, at #28, tel. 218-879-401) and the divey **Largo Café Estudio** (closed Mon, live music every Thu night, at #16).

Shopping is enjoyable here, especially at the flagship branch of **A Vida Portuguesa**—a stylish boutique celebrating made-in-Portugal gifts that feels a bit mainstream amid all this edginess (daily, on the square at #23). Next door—in the lavishly *azulejo*-slathered building at #25—is **Viúva Lamego,** selling quality Portuguese tiles (closed Sat-Sun—for more on both stores, see "Shopping in Lisbon").

If you want a bite beyond the basic light fare at the cafés on the square, along the main street is **$$$ Cervejaria Ramiro**—an old-school but newly in-vogue restaurant serving well-respected seafood and steak. It's hugely popular and becoming quite touristy—you can't miss the long line out front—but it's still a good choice (Tue-Sun 12:00-24:00, closed Mon, Avenida Almirante Reis 1H, tel. 218-851-024).

Evening Stroll

While not as big a deal as in Spain, the people of Lisbon enjoy a paseo-like early evening stroll after work and before dinner when the weather is balmy. When it comes to weather, Lisboners are pretty spoiled. If it's even a little blustery, they'll likely stay in. But when it's nice, in the summer, you'll find lots of people out strolling. Here are four good places to join them: Rua Augusta through the heart of the Baixa district; along the seaside promenade near Belém Tower; along the fine riverfront promenade at Parque das Nações; and the river walk at Ribeira das Naus (from the water at Praça do Comércio to Cais do Sodré).

FADO MUSIC

Fado is the ▲▲ folk music of Lisbon's back streets. Since the mid-1800s, it's been the Lisbon blues—mournfully beautiful and haunting ballads about lost sailors, broken hearts, and bittersweet romance. While generally sad, fado can also be jaunty—in a nostalgic way—and captivating. A stout 60-year-old widow singing fado can be invitingly sexy.

While authentically traditional, most Lisbon fado bars cater to tourists these days. Don't expect to find a truly "local" scene. Even the seemingly homemade "fado tonight" *(fado esta noite)* signs are mostly for tourist shows. Still, if you choose well—and can find a convivial restaurant with relatively reasonable prices and fewer tour groups—it's a very memorable evening. (And be wary of your hotel's recommendations, which are often skewed by hefty kick-backs.)

The two main areas for fado in Lisbon are on either side of the Baixa: the Bairro Alto and the Alfama. Below, I've listed options in each neighborhood. For locations, see the maps on page 110 and page 116. To avoid disappointment, it's smart to reserve ahead.

Ways to See Fado: Your basic choices are a polished restaurant with a professional-quality staged show; or—my preference—a more rustic place with *fado vadio,* a kind of open-mic fado evening when suspiciously talented "amateurs" line up at the door of neighborhood dives for their chance to warble. Waiters—hired more for their vocal skills than hospitality—sometimes take a turn entertaining the crowd.

Most people combine fado with a late dinner. The music typically begins between 20:00 and 21:00; arrive a bit earlier to be seated and order. Night owls can have a cheaper dinner elsewhere, then show up for fado when the first round of diners are paying their bills (around 22:30 or 23:00). Both elegant, high-end places and holes-in-the-wall generally let nondiners in late for the cost of an overpriced drink and/or a €10-15 cover charge.

Prices for Fado: Prices for a fado performance vary greatly, but assume you won't leave any fado experience without spending at least €30 per person—and more like €50-60 per person for the fancier restaurants. Many places have a cover charge, others just expect you to buy a steeply priced meal, and some enforce a €25-30 per person minimum. Remember, as throughout Portugal, appetizers, bread, or cheese that appear on your table aren't free—if you don't want these (exorbitantly priced) appetizers, it's safest to send them back.

Fado in the Bairro Alto

In the Bairro Alto, wander around Rua Diario de Noticias and neighboring streets.

Canto do Camões, while touristy, is romantic, candlelit, and classic. Run by friendly, English-speaking Gabriel, it's easy to reserve and has good music and tasty food. Call ahead to assure a seat. When it's busy, the room feels like a stage show, with 25 or 30 tables all enjoying classic fado. Relax, spend some time, and

Fado

Fado songs reflect Portugal's bittersweet relationship with the sea. Fado means "fate"—how fate deals with Portugal's adventurers...and the women they leave behind. These are songs of both sadness and hope, a bittersweet emotion called *saudade* (meaning yearning or nostalgia). The lyrics reflect the pining for a loved one across the water, hopes for a future reunion, remembrances of a rosy past or dreams of a better future, and the yearning for what might have been if fate had not intervened. (Fado can also be bright and happy when the song is about the virtues of cities such as Lisbon or Coimbra, or of the warmth of a typical *casa portuguesa*.)

The songs are often in a minor key. The singer *(fadista)* is accompanied by a 12-string Portuguese *guitarra* (with a round body like a mandolin) or other stringed instruments unique to Portugal. Many singers crescendo into the first word of the verse, like a moan emerging from deep inside. Though the songs are often sad, the singers rarely overact—they plant themselves firmly and sing stoically in the face of fate.

A verse from a typical fado song goes:

> O waves of the salty sea,
> where do you get your salt?
> From the tears shed by the women in black
> on the beaches of Portugal.

close your eyes, or make eye contact with the singer. Let the music and wine collaborate (open at 20:00, music from 20:30 until after midnight; no cover but €27 meal required—includes appetizer, 3 courses, water, and wine; after 22:00 €12 minimum for two drinks; from Rua da Misericordia, go 2 blocks uphill on Travessa da Espera to #38; tel. 213-465-464, www.cantodocamoes.pt).

Restaurante Adega do Ribatejo is a homey place crowded with locals and tourists nightly (except Sun) from around 20:00 to 24:00. It's just around the corner from Canto do Camões, and less touristy. This is a good budget alternative: just pay for your meal (main courses around €15) and drinks with no cover or required minimum (Mon-Sat from 19:00, closed Sun, Rua Diario de Noticias 23, tel. 213-468-343). After 22:30, you're welcome to just buy a drink and enjoy the music.

O Faia is a top-end fado experience, in a classy dining room under heavy, graceful arches. It's pricey (plan on €60/person for dinner and drinks), but the food and the fado are both professional and top-quality. If you come after dinner (23:00) for just drinks and music, there's a €25 minimum. Filled with an older, well-dressed, international clientele, it's a memorable evening (open Mon-Sat for dinner at 20:00, fado begins at 21:30, closed Sun, Rua da Barroca 54-56, tel. 213-426-742, www.ofaia.com).

Concert Alternative: Fado in Chiado, a sterile 50-minute performance in a small modern theater, is for tourists who don't want to stay out late or mess with a restaurant. Sitting with other tourists and without food or drink, you'll enjoy four musicians: a man and a woman singing, a guitarist, and a man on the Portuguese guitar, which gives fado its balalaika charm (€17, daily at 19:00 except Sun, conveniently located in Chiado at Rua da Misericordia 14, on second floor of in Cine Theatro Gymnasio, tel. 961-717-778, www.fadoinchiado.com).

Trendier Alternative: In the hip Pink Street nightlife zone, just downhill from the Bairro Alto and Chiado toward the river, **Povo Lisboa** has fado most nights (closed Mon, see listing on page 93).

Fado in the Alfama

While often pretty lonely and dead after dark, the Alfama has several bars offering fado with their meals—just head uphill from the Fado Museum. Some bars are geared for tourists and tour groups, but others feel organic, spontaneous, and part of the neighborhood culture. While schedules at any particular place can be inconsistent, if you hike up Rua São Pedro de Alcântara to the Church of São Miguel, you'll hear the music wafting out from hole-in-the-wall eateries and be greeted by men hustling business for their fado restaurants. Generally, you simply pay for the meal and enjoy the music as included entertainment. If it's late and there's room, you can just buy a drink. For locations, see map on page 116.

A Baiuca, a tiny fun-loving restaurant, offers my favorite Alfama fado experience. A Baiuca—the name means a very rough tavern—packs people in and serves up spirited *fado vadio* (open mic for amateurs) with overpriced, basic food and lots of wine. As the English-speaking manager, Isabel, likes to say, "Fado needs wine." This intimate place is a neighborhood affair and has surround sound—as everyone seems to get into the music (€25 minimum—and be careful with the very pricey appetizers and bottles of wine that can push the bill much higher). If you come very late you can just buy a drink (music Thu-Mon 20:00-24:00, closed Tue-Wed, reservations smart, in the heart of the Alfama, just off Rua São Pedro up the hill from Fado Museum at Rua de São Miguel 20, tel. 218-867-284). When the door is closed, they're full, but you can peek at the action through the window around to the left.

Clube de Fado is much classier—one of the best places in town to hear quality fado. While expensive, there's not a bad seat in the house. Music plays nightly in this formal yet intimate setting. When busy, the musicians switch between two adjacent halls, giving waiters time to serve between sets, and diners get music about half the time (plan on €50/person for dinner with wine, plus €7.50 cover charge, meals from 20:00, dinner reservations required, music 21:30 until after midnight; after 23:00, pay just €10 cover plus cost of a drink; around corner from cathedral at Rua São João da Praça 94, tel. 218-852-704, www.clube-de-fado.com).

Casa de Linhares, a block downhill from Clube de Fado, offers similar quality fado and an even nicer space, with dinner served under the stone vaults of a 16th-century palace (€15 cover for music, plan about €40/person for dinner, music nightly from 20:00, after 22:00 just cover plus drink purchase, Beco dos Armazéns Do Linho 2, tel. 218-865-088, www.casadelinhares.com).

Concerts at the Fado Museum: At the base of the Alfama, the Fado Museum hosts occasional live, free concerts that let you focus on the music (check schedule at www.museudofado.pt). Taking in a show here, then having a budget dinner elsewhere, lets you enjoy Alfama fado on the cheap.

BULLFIGHTS, SOCCER, CONCERTS, AND MOVIES
Tickets to bullfights, concerts, and other events are sold at the green **ABEP kiosk** at the southern end of Praça dos Restauradores (daily 9:00-20:00).

▲Portuguese Bullfight
If you always felt sorry for the bull, this is Toro's Revenge: In a Portuguese bullfight, the matador is brutalized along with the bull. Lisbon hosts only about a dozen fights a year, but if you're in town for one, it's an unforgettable experience.

In Act I, the horseman *(cavaleiro)* skillfully plants four beribboned barbs in the bull's back while trying to avoid the leather-padded horns. The horses are the short, stocky Lusitano breed, with excellent balance. In Act II, a colorfully clad eight-man suicide squad (called *forçados*) enters the ring and lines up single file facing the bull. With testosterone sloshing everywhere, the leader taunts the bull—slapping his knees and yelling, *"touro!"*—then braces himself for a collision that can be heard all the way up in the cheap

seats. As he hangs onto the bull's head, his buddies pile on, trying to wrestle the bull to a standstill. Finally, one guy hangs on to *o touro*'s tail and "water-skis" behind him. (In Act III, the *ambulância* arrives.)

Unlike the Spanish *corrida de toros*, the bull is not killed in front of the crowd at the Portuguese *tourada*...but it is killed later. (Some brave bulls with only superficial wounds are spared to fight another day.) Spanish aficionados insist that Portuguese fights are actually crueler, since they humiliate the bull, rather than fight him as a fellow warrior. Animal-rights groups enliven the scene before each fight.

Fights are held at the **Campo Pequeno,** a spectacular, Moorish-domed brick structure that bears a resemblance to Madrid's bullring. The ring is small, so there are no bad seats. To sit nearly at ringside, try the cheapest *bancada* seats, on the generally half-empty and unmonitored main floor. Underneath the ring there's a shopping mall, and overhead there's a retractable roof for concerts. It hosts a variety of restaurants inside, including an Argentine steak restaurant. Maybe the beef served was in the ring earlier?

Cost and Hours: Tickets are always available at the door (€20-50); they're also sold at the ABEP kiosk on Praça dos Restauradores (10 percent surcharge). Fights are generally held from Easter through September, typically on Thursday evenings at 22:00; bullring is north of the Baixa in the Campo Pequeno district (M: Campo Pequeno); tel. 217-932-143, www.campopequeno.com.

Important note: Half the fights are simply Spanish-type *corridas* without the killing. For the real slam-bam Portuguese-style fight, confirm that there will be *grupo de forçados* ("bull grabbers").

Soccer

Lisbon is home to two *futebol* teams, Benfica and Sporting CP, which means there are lots of games (1-2/week Aug-May, tickets €20 and up) and lots of team spirit. Benfica, with the red jerseys, plays at the 65,400-seat Stadium of Light, north of the city center (Estádio da Luz; M: Colegio Militar/Luz, www.slbenfica.pt). Sporting CP, with the green-and-white jerseys, plays at the 50,000-seat Estádio José Alvalade, which is also north of Lisbon's center (M: Campo Grande, www.sporting.pt). Tickets are generally available at the stadiums or at the ABEP kiosk on Praça dos Restauradores.

Concerts

The Gulbenkian Museum runs a classical concert season with about 180 events a year (www.gulbenkian.pt/musica; see page 56). You can hear classical music by national and city orchestras at the cultural center in Belém (www.ccb.pt). Traditional Portuguese theater plays in the National Theater on Rossio and in theaters along Rua das Portas de Santo Antão (the "eating lane"—see page 112) stretching north from Rossio. For popular music, these days you're more likely to find rock, jazz, Brazilian, and African music than traditional fado (which is more for tourists). The monthly *Agenda Cultural* provides the most up-to-date listing of world music, arts, and entertainment (free at TI, €0.50 at newsstands, online at www.agendalx.pt, in Portuguese only).

Movies

In Lisbon, unlike in Spain, most films are shown in the original language with subtitles. (That's one reason the Portuguese speak better English than the Spanish.) Many of Lisbon's theaters are classy, complete with assigned seats, ushers, and intermissions. The top places don't allow eating or drinking in the theater. Check the newspaper or online to see what's playing. Modern options are in malls like El Corte Inglés (M: São Sebastião) or at the Monumental complex in the ritzy Saldanha neighborhood (M: Saldanha).

Sleeping in Lisbon

Lisbon has a wide variety of accommodations. I've focused on a few categories: chic, international-style hotels offering a comfortable refuge at a high price; cheap, dingy, but affordable and safe old guesthouses (often up creaky old staircases in grimy buildings); newer boutique hotels offering a compromise between cost and comfort; and some famously classy hostels, which welcome travelers of all ages. For locations of accommodations, see the map on page 104.

Lisbon has become increasingly popular, and rates have increased accordingly—especially on weekends (Thu-Sun), when many Brits and other Europeans fly in for brief urban vacations. Conventions can clog Lisbon at any time, and the busiest time is during the Festas de Lisboa (the last three weeks of June)—when parades, street parties, concerts, and fireworks draw crowds to the city.

IN THE BAIXA

Central as can be, the grid-planned, easy-to-navigate Baixa district bustles with shops, traffic, tourists, commuters, street musicians, pedestrian areas, and urban intensity. It's close to Rossio station, and the Aerobus to and from the airport cuts right through its middle. And it's handy to all of your sightseeing—wedged between the Alfama and the Bairro Alto/Chiado, with vintage trolleys zipping through every few minutes.

Upscale Hotels

$$$$ My Story Hotel Rossio rents 46 well-equipped, stylish, efficient rooms in a couldn't-be-better location, tucked behind a strip of cafés facing bustling Rossio (air-con, elevator, Praça Dom Pedro IV 59, tel. 213-400-380, www.mystoryhotels.com, fom.rossio@mystoryhotels.com).

$$$$ Internacional Design Hotel has 55 small, chic rooms centrally located at the southeast corner of Rossio. Each of its four floors has a different theme—pop, Zen, tribal, and urban. Having breakfast in their expansive restaurant overlooking Rossio is a fine way to start the day (air-con, elevator, underground pay parking nearby, Rua da Betesga 3, tel. 213-240-990, www.idesignhotel.com, book@idesignhotel.com.

$$$$ Hotel Avenida Palace, the most characteristic five-star splurge in town, was built with Rossio station in 1892 to greet big-shot travelers. Back then, trains were new, and Rossio was the only station in town. The lounges are sumptuous, dripping with chandeliers, and the 82 rooms—while a bit faded—still mix elegance with modern comforts (air-con, elevator, free parking, hotel's sign is on Praça dos Restauradores but entrance is at Rua 1 de Dezembro 123—down a small alleyway next to Starbucks, tel. 213-218-121, www.hotelavenidapalace.pt, reservas@hotelavenidapalace.pt).

$$$ My Story Hotel Ouro has 51 rooms decorated in gold tones—*ouro* in Portuguese. Outside-facing rooms have great views over the busy Baixa streets below, but for maximum quiet, ask for an inside room (air-con, elevator, Rua Áurea 100, tel. 213-400-340, www.mystoryhotels.com, ouro@mystoryhotels.com).

Dumpy but Affordable Dives

Basically a notch up from a hostel, these are worth considering if you're on a tight budget and want a handy Baixa location. Keep in mind that you get what you pay for—these are the best I've found in this price bracket.

$ Pensão Praça da Figueira is a backpacker place on a quiet back street with youth-hostel prices, a kitchen on every floor, a slick modern lobby overlooking Praça da Figueira, and 32 basic but colorfully updated rooms—some with views on the square (cheaper rooms have shared bath but no air-con, 2 flights up with no elevator, entrance is at Travessa Nova de São Domingos 9, tel. 213-426-757, www.pensaopracadafigueira.com, pensaofigueira@clix.pt).

$ Residencial Florescente rents 67 straightforward rooms on the thriving, traffic-free "eating lane," a block off Praça dos Restauradores (air-con, elevator, Rua das Portas de Santo Antão 99, tel. 213-426-609, www.residencialflorescente.com, geral@residencialflorescente.com).

$ Pensão Residencial Gerês is a throwback, renting 20 well-worn, no-frills rooms with double-paned windows. The sweet Nogueira family speaks some English (RS%, cheaper rooms with private bathroom down the hall, no breakfast, uphill a block off

LISBON

Sleep Code

Hotels are classified based on the average price of a standard double room with breakfast in high season.

$$$$	**Splurge:** Most rooms over €150
$$$	**Pricier:** €100-150
$$	**Moderate:** €70-100
$	**Budget:** €40-70
¢	**Backpacker:** Under €40
RS%	**Rick Steves discount**

Unless otherwise noted, credit cards are accepted, hotel staff speak basic English, and free Wi-Fi is available. Comparison-shop by checking prices at several hotels (on each hotel's own website, on a booking site, or by email). For the best deal, *book directly with the hotel*. Ask for a discount if paying in cash; if the listing includes **RS%**, request a Rick Steves discount.

northeast corner of Rossio, Calçada do Garcia 6, tel. 215-958-368, no website but book at www.booking.com, infogereslx@gmail.com).

Boutique Hostels in the Baixa

Among hostel aficionados, Lisbon is famous for having the best hostels anywhere. They welcome travelers of any age, come with an artistic flair, and, besides the usual dorm beds, have plenty of double rooms (except Home Lisbon Hostel). These come with extras like bike rental, movie nights, and cheap or "free" (tip-based) city tours and excursions out of town.

¢ Lisbon Destination Hostel feels designed for backpackers—young and old—who appreciate style, peace, and quiet. Located upstairs in the Rossio train station (literally next to the platforms), it provides a wonderful value and experience. The astroturfed lounge—with beanbag chairs and hammocks—sprawls beneath an Industrial Age glass canopy (many private rooms available, movie night in lounge, Largo do Duque de Cadaval 17, tel. 213-466-457, www.destinationhostels.com, lisbon@destinationhostels.com).

¢ Home Lisbon Hostel is a little more rough and homey, with a loose camaraderie and friendly management. The hostel is dominated by its classic old wooden bar—an inviting place to socialize (all dorms—no private rooms, on the second floor at Rua de São Nicolau 13, near corner of Rua dos Fanqueiros, M: Baixa-Chiado, tel. 218-885-312, www.homelisbonhostel.com, info@homelisbonhostel.com).

¢ Living Lounge Hostel is clean, modern, and centrally located near the Baixa-Chiado Metro stop. Each room is uniquely decorated (private rooms including singles, some rooms with air-

con, Rua Crucifixo 116, second floor, tel. 213-461-078, www.
livingloungehostel.com, info@livingloungehostel.com).

¢ **Lisbon Lounge Hostel,** run by the same folks as the Living
Lounge Hostel above, is roughly midway between Praça da Figueira and Praça do Comércio (private rooms but no singles, Rua de
São Nicolau 41, tel. 213-462-061, www.lisbonloungehostel.com,
info@lisbonloungehostel.com).

IN THE CHIADO

The Chiado district feels like Lisbon's "uptown." For many, it's the
best of all worlds: It's handy to the Baixa and Rossio area (just
a few steps downhill), and to the artfully seedy Bairro Alto fado
zone (just a few steps uphill), but it feels less touristy and congested
than either. It's also a prime location for Lisbon's up-and-coming
foodie restaurants and hipster shopping scene, making this a fun
place simply to wander, graze, and window-shop. If I were buying
an apartment in Lisbon...I'd look in the Chiado. This area specializes in fresher, small, conscientiously run boutique hotels—often
upstairs in big buildings without elevators (expect lots of stairs).

$$$$ Casa Balthazar is an enticing splurge—an oasis-like
private compound of stately old townhouses tucked amid characteristic, restaurant-lined stepped lanes just above Rossio, on the
way up into the heart of the Chiado. Classy and modern but still
homey, each of its 17 rooms is different—some with views, terraces,
and/or private whirlpool baths. There's an inviting little swimming
pool, and breakfast is served in your room (air-con, Rua do Duque
26, mobile 917-085-568, www.casabalthazarlisbon.com, reservas@
casabalthazarlisbon.com).

$$$$ Lisboa Carmo Hotel is bigger and has less personality than the others listed here, but it's in an appealing location: a
few steps from the Chiado's charming Largo do Carmo. It has 45
sleek, straightforward, business-class rooms, not much in the way
of public spaces, and the only elevator among my Chiado listings
(air-con, elevator, Rua da Oliveira ao Carmo 1A, tel. 213-264-710,
carmo.luxhotels.pt, carmo.reservas@luxhotels.pt). Their newer sister property, **$$$$ Lisboa Pessoa Hotel,** has similar rooms and a
swimming pool just up the street in a neatly tiled building.

$$$ Casa do Barão is a delightful little refuge on a tame side-
street just a block below the bustling Praça Luís de Camões in the
heart of the Chiado. Its 12 tidy, well-appointed, modern rooms
share several fine common spaces, including a cozy library, win-
ter-garden breakfast room, gravel patio, and tiny swimming pool.
Complimentary coffee, tea, and snacks are available all day. At the
lower end of this price range, it's a terrific value and a comfortable
home base in Lisbon. As it's not staffed 24 hours a day, confirm

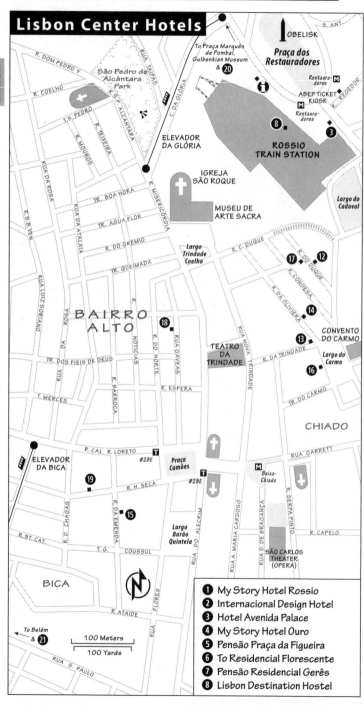

Lisbon Center Hotels

LISBON

OBELISK

Praça dos Restauradores

To Praça Marquês de Pombal, Gulbenkian Museum & 20

S. ANT.

R. DOM PEDRO V

R. S.P. ALCÂNTARA

RUA TAIPAS

R. COELHO

São Pedro de Alcântara Park

R. S. PEDRO

T. S. PEDRO

R. TEIXEIRA

R. MOUSOS

C. DA GLÓRIA

ELEVADOR DA GLÓRIA

Restauradores — M

ABEP TICKET KIOSK

Restauradores — M

8

3

R. REGEDOR

ROSSIO TRAIN STATION

Largo do Cadoval

IGREJA SÃO ROQUE

MUSEU DE ARTE SACRA

RUA DA ROSA

TR. BOA HORA

TR. AGUA FLOR

R. DA ATALAIA

K.S.B. VEN.

R. DO GREMIO

TR. QUEIMADA

Largo Trindade Coelho

R. C. DUQUE

17 R. DO DUQUE 12

R. CONDESA

R. DA OLIVEIRA

14

RUA LUIZ SORIANO

BAIRRO ALTO

R. DA ROSA

TR. DOS FIEIS DE DEUS

R. DO NORTE

NOTICIAS

RUA GAVEAS

18

RUA NOVA TRINDADE

TEATRO DA TRINDADE

13

CONVENTO DO CARMO

Largo do Carmo

16

R. DA TRINDADE

R. DO CARMO

CHIADO

RUA DA ROSA

R. BARROCA

R. ESPERA

T. MERCES

ELEVADOR DA BICA

R. CAL. R. LORETO

#28E T

Praça Camões

#28E T

RUA GARRETT

M Baixa-Chiado

19

R. H. SECA

R. DA EMENDA

15

R. D. CHAGAS

R. ST. CAT.

T. G. COUSSUL

Largo Barão Quintela

RUA DO ALECRIM

RUA A. MARIA CARDOSO

RUA D. DE BRAGANÇA

R. SERPA PINTO

R. CAPELO

SÃO CARLOS THEATER (OPERA)

BICA

R. ATAIDE

FLORES

RUA

To Belém & 21

100 Meters

100 Yards

❶ My Story Hotel Rossio
❷ Internacional Design Hotel
❸ Hotel Avenida Palace
❹ My Story Hotel Ouro
❺ Pensão Praça da Figueira
❻ To Residencial Florescente
❼ Pensão Residencial Gerês
❽ Lisbon Destination Hostel

RUA S. PAULO

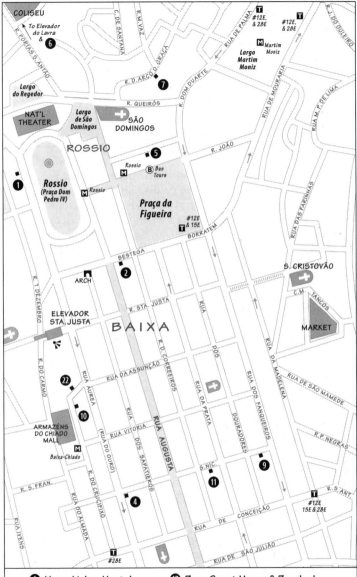

9 Home Lisbon Hostel
10 Living Lounge Hostel
11 Lisbon Lounge Hostel
12 Casa Balthazar
13 Lisboa Carmo Hotel
14 Lisboa Pessoa Hotel
15 Casa do Barão
16 Feeling Chiado 15

17 Zuza Guest House & Zuzabed
& Breakfast
18 Zuzabed Lisbon Suites
19 Chiado 44
20 To Avenida da Liberdade Area Hotels
21 To Hotel As Janelas Verdes
22 Laundry

your arrival details (air-con, Rua da Emenda 84, mobile 967-944-143, www.casadobarao.com, casasdobarao@gmail.com).

$$$ Feeling Chiado 15 is a fourth-floor walk-up with eight rooms high above the Chiado's most appealing little leafy square, Largo do Carmo. Four of the rooms—at the cheaper end of this price range—look down over a residential patio; the pricier, "deluxe" rooms have views over Lisbon's rooftops and castle (most rooms have air-con, Largo do Carmo 15, tel. 213-470-845, www.feelingchiado.com, feelingchiado@gmail.com).

Zuza, run by entrepreneurial Luis Zuzarte, has rooms in three different buildings around the Chiado. The main branch, **$ Zuza Guest House,** has eight basic but neatly outfitted rooms with shared bathrooms in a creaky old building (no air-con, Rua do Duque 41). A few doors down, **$$ Zuzabed & Breakfast** has four rooms with bathrooms and castle views (air-con, Calçada do Duque 29). And a short walk away, up in the Bairro Alto, **$$$ Zuzabed Lisbon Suites** has seven classy rooms with vintage furnishings (Rua das Gáveas 81). Let them know when you'll arrive: If coming in the morning, you'll likely check in at the Rua do Duque location, but in the afternoon you'll head to the location you're sleeping at (contact for all: mobile 934-445-500, www.zuzabed.com, zuzabed@zuzabed.com).

$$ Chiado 44 is a simple place in a great location, just below Praça Luís de Camões. Its 11 small, basic, but comfortable rooms fill a historic building—expect plenty of stairs (air-con, Rua Horta Seca 44, mobile 918-352-901, www.chiado44.pt, info@chiado44.pt, Fabian).

ALONG AVENIDA DA LIBERDADE

Avenida da Liberdade is an upscale neighborhood facing a broad, tree-lined, very European-feeling boulevard. Most of my listings are a block or so off the main street. While it's a residential area, there are also lots of hotels—it's where many of Lisbon's tourists go to sleep. For this reason, it's a bit less characteristically "Lisbon" than some other neighborhoods...but for the sake of a quiet night's sleep, some consider that a good thing. These listings are a 10-minute walk or short Metro ride from the center. Most are near the Avenida Metro stop; Lisbon Dreams is closer to the Rato station.

High-End Chain Hotels

The **Hoteis Heritage Lisboa** chain has several branches, most near Avenida da Liberdade. These hotels distinguish themselves with classy public spaces and rooms, professional staff, and top-notch amenities (air-con, elevator, pay parking); guests are entitled to sightseeing deals—ask for details. Each hotel has its own style and personality (website for all: www.heritage.pt).

$$$$ Hotel Britania maintains its 1940s Art Deco charm throughout its 33 spacious rooms, offering a clean and professional haven on a workaday street one block off Avenida da Liberdade. Three top-floor rooms are decorated in a luxurious Mod Deco style (Rua Rodrigues Sampaio 17, tel. 213-155-016, britania.hotel@ heritage.pt).

$$$$ Heritage Avenida Liberdade is the most contemporary, the only one actually on the leafy boulevard, and the closest to the center (a 5-minute walk from Rossio). Its stylish lobby/breakfast room is inviting, and the 42 rooms feel upscale-urban (Avenida da Liberdade 28, tel. 213-404-040, avliberdade@heritage.pt).

$$$$ Hotel As Janelas Verdes is farther out—west of the center, next door to the Museum of Ancient Art, filling an 18th-century mansion with 29 cushy rooms and comfortably elegant public spaces. The third-floor library overlooks the river (Rua das Janeles Verdes 7, bus #714 stops nearby, tel. 213-968-143, janelas. verdes@heritage.pt).

$$$ Hotel Lisboa Plaza—a large, plush gem—mixes traditional style with bright-pastel classiness. Its 112 rooms are on a quiet street off busy Avenida da Liberdade, a block from the Avenida Metro station (free port wine after 18:00, Travessa do Salitre 7, tel. 213-218-218, plaza@heritage.pt).

Other Avenida Liberdade Hotels

$$$ Hotel Alegria faces a quiet, inviting park in a peaceful neighborhood 200 yards from the Avenida Metro station. Its bright, inviting public spaces and 30 comfortable, well-appointed rooms have hardwood floors varnished like a ship's deck (breakfast extra, air-con, elevator, Praça da Alegria 12, tel. 213-220-670, www. hotelalegria.pt, info@hotelalegria.pt).

$ Lisbon Dreams Guest House has 18 fresh, relaxing, Ikea-style rooms, occupying three apartments and sharing seven bathrooms (shared kitchen and terraces; M: Marquês de Pombal, then take Rua Alexandre Herculano uphill and turn left on Rua Rodrigo da Fonesca, or M: Rato, take Rua Alexandre Herculano downhill, then right to reach Rua Rodrigo da Fonesca 29, tel. 213-872-393, www.lisbondreams.com, info@lisbondreams.com).

Eating in Lisbon

Each district of the city comes with fun and characteristic restaurants. (Good eateries in Belém are described on page 67.) Ideally, have one dinner with a fado performance—several good options for music with your meal are listed in this section, with more fado options described earlier, under "Entertainment in Lisbon." Note that some smaller, family-run places take a few weeks off in the late summer or early fall—don't be surprised to find a handwritten *fechado para férias* (closed for vacation) sign taped to the window.

Snack Bars: Lisbon seems enthusiastic about serving quick, light meals at characteristic bars. On just about any street, you can belly up to a bar, observe, and order what looks good for a tasty, memorable, and extremely cheap meal. You'll see lots of *pastel de bacalhau,* Lisbon's ubiquitous and delicious cod cake. Other good standbys are *prego* (steak sandwich) and *bifana* (pork sandwich), each made with a secret sauce to give them character.

Food Tours in Lisbon: To simultaneously eat good food, learn about Portuguese cuisine, and meet a knowledgeable local guide, consider taking one of the food tours (described on page 20). These tours are informative, tasty, and a good value—filling you in while filling you up.

IN THE BAIXA
Near Rossio

My first few listings here are nice, sit-down eateries, while the rest are good for a quick bite. The area around Rossio station, with plenty of practical, inexpensive eateries, caters to busy locals commuting in and out by train.

$$$ Bastardo Restaurante—upstairs in the recommended Internacional Design Hotel—is a simple, solid, no-stress option for Portuguese cuisine with a modern twist overlooking the square. The space is fresh, bright, and accessible, like the menu. It can be smart to reserve (vegan options, daily 12:30-15:00 & 19:30-23:00, Rua da Betesga 3, facing Rossio, tel. 213-240-993, http://restaurantebastardo.com).

$$$$ Pinóquio Restaurante, a venerable seafood beer hall famous for its clams (€22 splittable portion), has a good local energy. You'll dine with a smart crowd at white-tableclothed tables yet with no pretense—the focus is on simple quality (daily 12:00-24:00, big portions, dine inside or outside facing the busy square, Praça dos Restauradores 79, tel. 213-465-106).

$$ Confeitaria Nacional has been proudly satisfying sweet tooths for 180 years, and was once the favorite of Portuguese royalty. Stop in for a tasty pastry downstairs. Or, for a peaceful and inexpensive lunch, go upstairs, where you'll choose between a cheaper meal in the cafeteria or pay a little extra for service and Old World sophistication in the elegant dining room (Mon-Sat 8:00-20:00, pastry counter open Sun but upstairs may be closed, Praça da Figueira 18, tel. 213-424-470).

$ Restaurante Beira-Gare is my choice for a quick, cheap meal immediately across the street from Rossio station. A classic greasy-spoon diner, it dishes out cod and vegetables prepared faster than a Big Mac and served with more energy than a soccer team.

Restaurant Price Code

I've assigned each eatery a price category, based on the average cost of a typical main course. Drinks, desserts, and splurge items (steak and seafood) can raise the price considerably.

$$$$	**Splurge:**	Most main courses over €17
$$$	**Pricier:**	€12-17
$$	**Moderate:**	€7-12
$	**Budget:**	Under €7

In Portugal, takeout food is **$**; a basic sit-down eatery is **$$**; a casual but more upscale restaurant is **$$$**; and a swanky splurge is **$$$$**.

The house specialty is a pork sandwich *(bifana no pão)*. Consider their soup-and-sandwich special (Mon-Sat 6:00-24:00, closed Sun, stand at the bar or grab a table, Rua 1 de Dezembro, tel. 213-420-405).

$ Casa Brasileira offers a characteristic budget snack or meal in a classic local scene. Fast, cheap lunch deals are served only at the bar, or choose the sidewalk tables with a higher-priced menu. And their *pastel de nata* (custard tart), made downstairs, is as tasty as those that people line up for in Belém (daily 7:00-24:00, 100 yards from Rossio at Rua Augusta 265, tel. 213-459-713).

$ A Tendinha do Rossio, established in 1840 and run by Calheiros and Carmo, is a classic *ginjinha* bar that also sells soups, sandwiches, and fishy snacks. While it's pretty dumpy, it's notable because it offers the only cheap tables on Rossio. Prices are dirt-cheap and the same whether you sit with the drunks at the bar, grab a tiny table inside, or serve yourself and sit outside overlooking Rossio (Mon-Sat 7:00-21:00, closed Sun, Praça Dom Pedro IV 6, tel. 213-468-156).

Rua 1 de Dezembro: This street, which is active during the workday and dead after hours, is lined with cheap restaurants that make self-service speed a priority for busy office workers who eat here. Walk the street from Rossio station to the Elevador de Santa Justa to determine the prevailing menu of the day. **$$ Leão d'Ouro** has a fancy and expensive sit-down restaurant, but their handy self-service cafeteria next door (at #97) offers an affordable lunch or dinner buffet (daily 12:00-23:00). There are also two grocery stores on this street (open long hours daily): the straightforward **Pingo Doce supermarket** (at #73, with very cheap 9-stool cafeteria), and—across the street—the organic/health-food alternative, **Celeiro,** which also has a self-service vegetarian lunch joint (called Tasquinha do Celeiro, at #53, Mon-Fri 8:00-18:00, closed Sat-Sun).

$ Armazéns do Chiado Mall: The sixth-floor food court at

LISBON

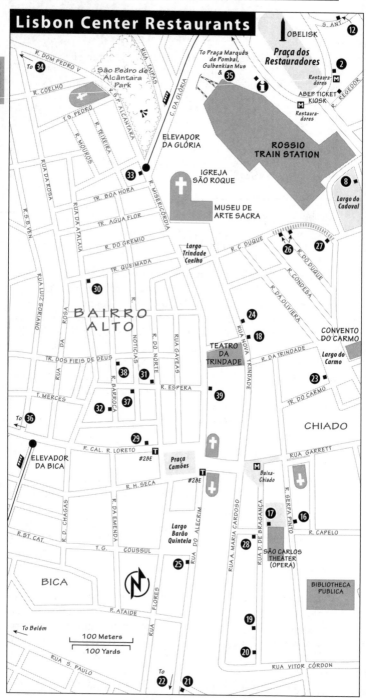

Lisbon Center Restaurants

S. ANT.

OBELISK

Praça dos Restauradores

To 34

R. DOM PEDRO V

São Pedro de Alcântara Park

To Praça Marquês de Pombal, Gulbenkian Mus & 35

Restauradores

ABEP TICKET KIOSK

Restauradores

R. COELHO

R. S. P. ALCÂNTARA

R. TEIXEIRA

R. MOIROS

T. S. PEDRO

R. DA ROSA

R. 5.B.VEN

ROSSIO TRAIN STATION

ELEVADOR DA GLÓRIA

33

IGREJA SÃO ROQUE

MUSEU DE ARTE SACRA

Largo do Cadoval

8

TR. BOA HORA

TR. ÁGUA FLOR

R. DO GRÉMIO

TR. QUEIMADA

R. DA ATALAIA

R. MISERICÓRDIA

Largo Trindade Coelho

R. C. DUQUE

26

27

R. DO DUQUE

R. CONDESA

RUA LUIZ SORIANO

BAIRRO ALTO

30

R. DA ROSA

R. DO NORTE

RUA GAVEAS

R. NOTÍCIAS

TR. DOS FIEIS DE DEUS

38

31

R. BARROCA

R. DA OLIVEIRA

R. DA TRINDADE

24

18

TEATRO DA TRINDADE

RUA NOVA TRINDADE

CONVENTO DO CARMO

Largo do Carmo

23

R. DO CARMO

R. ESPERA

39

TR. DO CARMO

T. MERCES

32

37

CHIADO

To 36

29

R. CAL. R. LORETO

#28E

ELEVADOR DA BICA

Praça Camões

#28E

RUA GARRETT

Baixa-Chiado

R. H. SECA

R. D. CHAGAS

R. DA EMENDA

Largo Barão Quintela

RUA DO ALECRIM

RUA MARIA CARDOSO

RUA A. MARIA CARDOSO

RUA D. DE BRAGANÇA

R. SERPA PINTO

17

16

R. CAPELO

R. ST. CAT.

T. G. COUSSUL

28

25

SÃO CARLOS THEATER (OPERA)

BICA

RUA FLORES

BIBLIOTHECA PUBLICA

To Belém

R. ATAIDE

100 Meters

100 Yards

19

20

To 22

21

RUA S. PAULO

RUA VITOR CÓRDON

To

1. Bastardo Restaurante
2. Pinóquio Restaurante
3. Confeitaria Nacional
4. Restaurante Beira-Gare
5. Casa Brasileira
6. A Tendinha do Rossio
7. Rua 1 de Dezembro Eateries
8. Leão d'Ouro Rest./Café
9. Pingo Doce Supermarket
10. Celeiro
11. Armazéns do Chiado Mall Eateries
12. Bonjardim Restaurante
13. Casa do Alentejo Restaurante/Bar
14. To Rest. Solar dos Presuntos & Cantinho São José
15. To Nova Pombalina
16. Belcanto
17. Café Lisboa
18. Bairro do Avillez
19. Cantinho do Avillez
20. Pizzaria Lisboa
21. Restaurante Vicente
22. To "Pink Street" Nightlife
23. Carmo Restaurante & Bar
24. Cervejaria da Trindade
25. By the Wine
26. Café Buenos Aires & Solar do Duque
27. El Rei D'Frango
28. Café no Chiado
29. Manteigaria
30. Restaurante Bota Alta
31. A Primavera do Jerónimo & Canto do Camões Rest. & Fado
32. Lisbon Winery
33. Solar do Vinho do Porto
34. To Príncipe Real Garden Eateries
35. To Cervejaria Ribadouro & Restaurante A Gina
36. To Mercado de Campo de Ourique
37. Restaurante Adega do Ribatejo Fado
38. O Faia Fado
39. Fado in Chiado
40. Wines of Portugal Tasting Room
41. To Martinho da Arcada Café Bar

LISBON

Lisbon's Gourmet Food-Circus Markets

The big news on Lisbon's eating scene is the transformation of traditional farmers markets into gourmet food circuses. These combine the stalls of traditional food-market vendors (selling produce, meat, fish, spices, etc.) with a food court filled with eateries run by locally respected chefs. If you love food—or even if you don't—these are fun to explore.

Mercado da Ribeira (a.k.a. Time Out Market)

Located at Cais do Sodré (between the Chiado and the river), this is two markets in one: The boisterous and venerable market survives in one half of the Industrial Age, iron-and-glass market hall, while the other half has become a trendy food court curated by *Time Out* magazine, which has invited a few dozen quality restaurants to open outposts here. Eating here on disposable plates and long, noisy picnic tables is far from romantic, but the quality and prices are great. The produce and fish market is open from 7:00 to 13:00 (closed Sun and no fish Mon), while the restaurants are open daily from 12:00 to 24:00. This place is no secret—to avoid a mob scene at dinnertime, arrive before 19:00.

Getting There: The Mercado da Ribeira (like many locals, I resist calling this venerable market by its new "Time Out" name) is across the street from the Cais do Sodré train station. It's conveniently served by the Metro (Cais do Sodré stop) and tram #15E (on the way to/from Belém), and it's about a 10-minute walk from Praça do Comércio. If you're here for dinner, note that the crazy Pink Street—lined with clubs and bars—is just two blocks inland and lively late (described in "Entertainment in Lisbon," earlier).

Eating at Mercado da Ribeira: Entering the market from the main entrance (facing Cais do Sodré), the workaday market

this shopping center, between the Bairro Alto and the Baixa, offers a selection of fun eateries—mostly fast food and chain restaurants you'd find in any modern mall, but a few are actual restaurants with castle views (daily 12:00-23:00, between Rua Garrett and Rua da Assunção; from the lower town, find the inconspicuous elevator at Rua do Crucifixo 89 or 113, next to the Baixa-Chiado Metro entrance). **$ Loja das Sopas** has hearty soups with cheap fixed-price meals. **$ Companhia das Sandes** offers up hearty sandwiches and healthy, big-bowl pasta salads topped with tropical fruits. **$$ Restaurant Chimarrão** serves Brazilian cuisine and offers an impressive *rodizio:* an all-you-can-eat buffet of salad, veggies, and endless beef, ham, pork, sausage, and chicken (€11 for weekday lunch, €13 for dinner and on weekends).

Lisbon's "Eating Lane"

Just north of Rossio, Rua das Portas de Santo Antão is Lisbon's stalls are on your right, while the foodie festival is on your left. In the food court, join the young, trendy, hungry, and thirsty crowd grazing among a wide variety of options. Assemble a sampling of local treats, and grab a seat at the big, shared tables in the middle. The north wall is a row of stalls run by big-name Lisbon chefs offering quality dishes at reasonable prices (enticing dinner plates for €10). And there are also branches of Honorato (a local "gourmet burger" chain), O Prego da Peixaria (fish and steak sandwiches), Sea Me (a Chiado institution for seafood), Aloma (in the west outer aisle, for the best pastries), and Santini (the venerable Portuguese gelateria). Get wine and beer from separate stalls in the center. You may find affordable *percebes* (barnacles) at several seafood stalls.

Mercado de Campo de Ourique

A trendy marketplace fills this 19th-century iron-and-glass market. Compared to Mercado da Ribera, it's less crowded and more purely local. Produce stalls, fishmongers, and bakeries sell everything from pigs' ears to fragrant bunches of cilantro (most close in the evening). At lunch and dinner, local diners pick up meals from whichever counter appeals: pork, seafood, Japanese, wine, beer, coffee, meat, produce, artisanal gelato, and so on (most eateries open daily 10:00-23:00).

Getting There: It's a couple of miles west of Rossio. Take a taxi or Uber, or hop on trolley #28E and ride to the second-to-last stop (Igreja Sto. Condestável; market is behind the big church). Lisbon's most interesting cemetery is one stop farther, at the end of the trolley line.

"eating lane"—a galaxy of eateries, many specializing in seafood (off the northeast corner of Rossio). While the waiters are pushy and it's all very touristy, the lane—lively with happy eaters—is enjoyable to browse. This is a fine spot to down a beer, snack on some snails, and watch people go by. The last two options are just beyond the end of the eating lane, and therefore less touristy (they're also handier to hotels on Avenida da Liberdade).

$$ Bonjardim, a family-friendly diner on a small side street, is known for its tasty rotisserie chicken—paint on some spicy African *piri-piri* sauce (Tue 19:00-23:00, Wed-Sun 12:00-23:00, closed Mon, Travessa do Santo Antão 7 or 10, both branches run by same owner, tel. 213-427-424).

$$$ Casa do Alentejo Restaurante specializes in Alentejo cuisine and fills an old, second-floor dining hall. The Moorish-looking building is a cultural and social center for transplants from the Alentejo, the traditional southern province of Portugal (and historically the poorest region in the country). While the food is mainly hearty and simple, come for the ambience. It's a good place to try regional specialties such as pork with clams, or the super-sweet, eggy almond dessert called *charcada*. The full-bodied Alentejo red wine is cheap and solid (lunch specials, Tue-Sun 12:00-15:00 & 19:00-22:00, Mon 19:00-22:00, slip into the closed-looking building at Rua das Portas de Santo Antão 58 and climb stairs to the right, tel. 213-469-231). They host folk singing in the grand ballroom (often on Sat from 15:00) and ballroom dancing (on many Sun from 15:00 to 19:00), except in summer when it's too hot (mid-June-mid-Sept).

$ Casa do Alentejo Bar, in the same building, serves cheap bar food and wine, either in the sleek-and-trendy interior or out on the little patio (spicy meat dishes, hearty cheeses, other tapas; daily 12:00-23:00, to the right of the stairs, look for *taberna* sign on main floor).

$$$$ Restaurante Solar dos Presuntos keeps the theater crowd happily fed with meat and seafood specialties. Its upstairs is more elegant, while the downstairs—with a colorful, open kitchen—is higher energy. Photos of Lisbon's celebrities and politicians who eat here enliven the walls. This place can take advantage of its popularity and bulldoze tourists into spending a lot—order cautiously and know what you're paying for. Reservations are smart (big splittable portions, good wine list, see daily suggestions, Mon-Sat 12:00-15:30 & 19:00-23:00, closed Sun, at the top end of Rua das Portas de Santo Antão at #150, tel. 213-424-253, www.solardospresuntos.com).

$ Cantinho São José is a wonderfully untouristy, cheap-and-cheery hole-in-the-wall a block beyond the main restaurant zone. Its extremely tight, tiled interior is jammed with tiny tables filled by big locals ordering hearty, splittable portions of Portuguese classics—for pennies on the dollar compared to the tourist traps nearby (Sun-Fri 9:00-24:00, closed Sat, Rusa São José 94, tel. 213-427-866).

Below the Cathedral

These places are at the southeast corner of the Baixa, on the way to the Alfama.

$ Nova Pombalina is a busy little joint that serves quick sandwiches, soups, and exotic fresh-squeezed juices. It's famous among office workers for its suckling pig sandwich *(sandes de leitão)*. They have good *piri-piri* sauce on request. From Praça do Comércio, it's five blocks toward the castle, on the corner of Rua do Comércio and Rua da Madalena (Mon-Sat 8:00-19:00, closed Sun, Rua do Comércio 2, for location see map on page 110, tel. 218-874-360).

$$ Mesa Kreol offers a lively taste of Portugal's former over-

Appetizers Aren't Free

Remember: In Portugal, there's no such thing as a free munch. Appetizers brought to your table before you order (such as olives, bread, and fancy pâtés) are not free. So if you don't want to pay for them, just push them aside or wave them away when the waiter brings them. Don't eat any of it—not even one olive—or you'll be charged (only €1-2 for the simpler appetizers, but it's disturbing if you don't expect it).

seas colonies—with cuisine from Cape Verde, Mozambique, Angola, and Brazil. Its interior is small, cozy, and nondescript, but the cuisine is a bold and flavorful change of pace. Manager Ju enjoys helping his guests navigate the menu, and there's often live music (Tue-Sun 19:00-24:00, closed Mon, Arco das Portas do Mar 29, for location see map on page 116, mobile 910-629-690).

IN THE ALFAMA

These are listed geographically, from just below the castle at the top to the Fado Museum at the bottom.

Lunch on Largo do Contador Mor: This leafy and picturesque square, just under the castle, has a few interchangeable **$$** restaurants serving up decent plates of grilled sardines *(sardinhas grelhadas)*. But the real star of the square is **$ Miss Can,** an engaging, colorful, and stylish little shop that's injecting some contemporary class into the beloved Portuguese tradition of canned fish. Three young, hip Lisboners have returned to their roots (their families have been in the sardine biz for generations) to create fresh new packaging for a variety of canned sardines, mackerel, and cod. Peruse their shop, and pick a can or two to eat with bread, salad, and a drink at one of their inviting little café tables (daily 11:00-19:00, at #17, mobile 910-007-004, www.miss-can.com).

Near the Santa Luzia Viewpoint: $$$ Farol de Santa Luzia, which offers a nice seafood feast with a delicate and delightful dining area, is a favorite of mine for dinner at the top of the Alfama. A family-run place with a local clientele, it offers the Algarve *cataplana* style of cooking—simmered in a copper pot (€27 big *cataplana* of meat, fish, or shellfish for two; indoor seating only, Mon-Sat 17:30-23:00, closed Sun, Largo Santa Luzia 5, across from Santa Luzia viewpoint terrace, tiny sign, tel. 218-863-884; Andre, Luis, and family).

Near Largo Rodrigues de Freitas: For more of an adventure with your meal, walk past Largo das Portas do Sol and follow the trolley tracks along Rua de São Tomé to a square called Largo Rodrigues de Freitas—if riding trolley #12E, it's the first stop over the big hill. On this square, **$$ Restaurante Frei Papinhas** is a

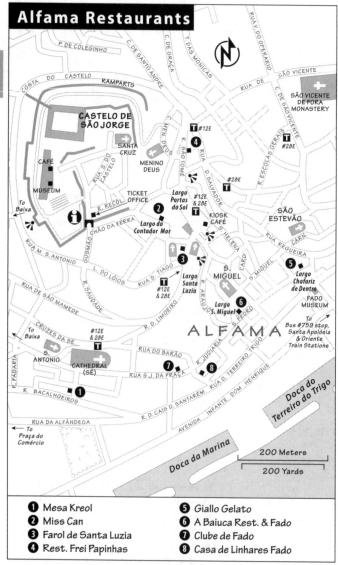

Alfama Restaurants

- **1** Mesa Kreol
- **2** Miss Can
- **3** Farol de Santa Luzia
- **4** Rest. Frei Papinhas
- **5** Giallo Gelato
- **6** A Baiuca Rest. & Fado
- **7** Clube de Fado
- **8** Casa de Linhares Fado

classic, family-run, hole-in-the-wall where you can feast on fresh seafood with the neighborhood crowd. Dine inside, or at rickety tables across the street in a charming square—where you can watch the trolleys rattle by (daily 12:00-16:00 & 19:00-24:00, Rua de São Tome 13, tel. 218-866-471).

Fado Deep in the Alfama: While the Bairro Alto is far livelier at night and has a better energy, the Alfama still has a unique charm. My favorite places for dinner with fado are described earlier, under "Entertainment in Lisbon."

Ice Cream: Giallo, across Campo de Ourique from the Fado Museum, has an enticing array of high-quality artisanal gelato.

IN THE CHIADO

The Chiado has some of Lisbon's trendiest restaurants. If you don't mind paying a bit more to experience the city's burgeoning food scene (rather than the old-school, fill-the-tank, and tourist-focused places in other neighborhoods), venture up into these inviting streets. When considering these listings, remember that the more traditional Bairro Alto neighborhood—covered in the next section—is just a few minutes' walk away.

José Avillez Restaurants: One of Portugal's top celebrity chefs, José Avillez, has elevated and modernized Portuguese classics with international influences and techniques. He runs a growing empire of pricey but excellent destination restaurants in Lisbon (reservations recommended for all; www.joseavillez.pt). His flagship location is the Michelin-starred **$$$$ Belcanto,** a top-end splurge (with €125-145 tasting *menus*, closed Sun-Mon, Largo de São Carlos 10, tel. 213-420-607). But other nearby locations offer far more affordable tastes. **$$$ Café Lisboa,** directly across the square from Belcanto (in front of the opera house), has indoor and outdoor seating, uneven service, and delicious modern Portuguese dishes (daily 12:00-24:00, Largo de São Carlos 23, tel. 211-914-498). A couple of blocks away, **Bairro do Avillez** is bright and boisterous. There's a lively **$$$** *taberna* up front with small plates, main courses, casual seating, and lots of well-dressed urbanites mingling at the bar; in back, the **$$$$** *páteo* under a glass skylight offers a full menu of pricier fish and seafood dishes (both open daily 12:00-24:00 but no meals served in *páteo* 15:30-19:00, Rua Nova da Trinidade 18, tel. 211-992-369). Two more, less expensive Avillez eateries are just downhill (toward the river) on Rua dos Duques de Bragança: **$$$ Cantinho do Avillez,** with a casual vibe and a more international menu (daily, at #7), and **$$$ Pizzaria Lisboa** (daily, at #5).

$$$ Restaurante Vicente, at the southern edge of the Chiado (downhill from the main zone, halfway to Mercado da Ribeira), fills a former brick-arched coal warehouse with rustic-trendy decor and excellent Alentejo cuisine from Portugal's arid southern heartland. The hearty, delicious meals come with real history: Traditionally, coal cellars like this one came with a crow named "Vicente" to act as an early-warning system for polluted air—like the proverbial canary in a coal mine (Mon-Fri 12:30-15:30 & 19:30-24:00, Sat-Sun 19:30-24:00, Rua das Flores 6, tel. 218-066-142).

$$ Carmo Restaurante and Bar offers delicious updated

Portuguese cooking. You can share a few *petiscos* (Portuguese-style tapas), or get well-presented main courses. In good weather, sit out on the inviting square, under a leafy canopy. Otherwise, take advantage of the chic-but-homey setting, with a series of smaller rooms that help you get away from the crowds (weekday lunch deals, tempting desserts, daily 12:00-23:00, Largo do Carmo 11, tel. 213-460-088).

$$$ Cervejaria da Trindade—a bright, boisterous, beer hall—is full of historic tiles, seafood, and tourists. While over-priced and in all the guidebooks, it's a historic landmark (see description on page 47). The seafood is charged by weight—clarify prices when you order (daily 12:00-24:00, liveliest 20:00-22:00, air-con, courtyard, a block down from São Roque Church at Rua Nova da Trindade 20C, tel. 213-423-506).

$$$ By the Wine is a trendy yet accessible wine bar, filling a cellar under a green-bottled vaulted ceiling. They serve a few dozen Portuguese wines by the glass, thoughtfully paired with local cold cuts and cheeses, small plates, and main dishes. It's less intimate and informative than Lisbon Winery (described later), but busier, more atmospheric, and more food-focused (Mon 18:00-24:00, Tue-Sun 12:00-24:00, Rua das Flores 41-43, tel. 213-420-319).

$$$ Café Buenos Aires is a friendly place serving Argentinian cuisine (lots of red meat), hearty dinner salads, vegetarian homemade pasta, and famous chocolate cake. Dine in the charming and intimate woody interior, or at fun tables outside on a characteristic, stepped pedestrian lane with views across to the Alfama (daily 18:00-24:00, Rua do Duque 31, tel. 213-420-739). Above this place and on the same lane is **$$ Solar do Duque,** a typical Portuguese eatery with romantic tables on the stepped lane (daily, Rua do Duque 67, tel. 213-426-901).

$ El Rei D'Frango ("King of Chicken") is a local favorite for huge portions of affordable, stick-to-your-ribs grilled meat and fish specialties (but, strangely, little to no chicken), served in an unpretentious little hole-in-the-wall. It's on the steep stepped lanes at the very bottom of the Chiado, just above the back end of the Baixa, behind Rossio station (Mon-Sat 10:00-22:00, closed Sun, Calçada do Duque 5, tel. 213-424-066).

$$$ Café no Chiado is perched on an upper street overlooking the square in front of the **São Carlos** opera house (find the stairs up next to the recommended Café Lisboa). It's a local favorite for its brief, accessible menu. The interior is casual-classy, and the outdoor tables—on a tiny square under red-and-black awnings—feels very European (daily 12:00-24:00, Largo do Picadeiro, tel. 213-460-502).

Dessert: $ Manteigaria is simply the best place in town for *pastel de nata*—everyone's favorite local pastry. They serve only this one treat, constantly churning the lovable little €1 custard pies out of the oven so you eat them not "reheated warm"...but literally hot from the oven. While here, enjoy a look at the busy little kitchen (daily until 24:00, Rua Loreto 2 just off Praça Camões).

IN THE BAIRRO ALTO

For a characteristic meal in Old World surroundings, the Bairro Alto is hard to beat.

Fado with Dinner in Bairro Alto: For a most memorable dining experience with live fado music in the Bairro Alto, consider **Canto do Camões** (more formal and subdued, Travessa da Espera 38), **Restaurante Adega do Ribatejo** (more rough and casual, Rua Diario de Noticias 23), or **O Faia** (top-end splurge with quality food and fado, Rua da Barroca 54-56). All are described under "Entertainment in Lisbon" on page 92; for locations, see map on page 110.

$$ Restaurante Bota Alta ("The Old Boot") is a classic—if a bit touristy—little eatery with a timeless Portuguese ambience, tight seating, and reliably good food. Portions are big, and Paulo offers a fun dessert sampler plate. Reservations are smart. (Mon-Sat 12:00-14:30, 19:00-23:00, closed Sun, at corner of Travessa da Queimada and Rua da Atalaia, tel. 213-427-959).

$$ A Primavera do Jerónimo is a quintessential Bairro Alto joint serving traditional home-style plates in a jam-packed, joyfully characteristic scene. Rafael and Helena love serving stuffed squid and Brás-style cod—whipped into a frittata with potatoes and onions (Mon-Sat opens at 19:30, closed Sun; reserve, come early, or wait; at Travessa da Espera 38, a few steps below recommended fado place Canto do Camões, tel. 213-420-477).

$$$ Lisbon Winery, a modern, casual little wine bar and tapas place, has a passion for the best wines, cheeses, and meats. With quality local ingredients, cork walls, and fado music playing, it's a perfect storm of Portuguese culture. Sommelier Alex is evangelical about Portuguese wines and ports, and how to complement them with tasty foods. Just tell him your budget, and he'll work within it. For a memorable and educational light meal, two people can pay €20 each for a complete array of cheeses, meats, and wines. Cap your experience by tossing a cork into the 500 year-old cistern (Tue-Sun 15:00-24:00, closed Mon, Rua da Barroca 13, tel. 218-260-132, www.lisbonwinery.com. They also do wine tastings (€50-60/person, typically at 15:30, but confirm).

Serious Port Wine Tastings

Solar do Vinho do Porto, run by the Port Wine Institute, has perhaps the world's greatest selection of port—the famous fortified wine that takes its name from the city of Porto. If you're not headed to Porto, this is your best chance for a serious lesson. The plush, air-conditioned, Old World living room is furnished with leather chairs (this is not a shorts-and-T-shirt kind of place). You can order from a selection of more than 150 different ports (€2-22/glass), generally poured by an English-speaking bartender. Read the instructive menu for an education in port. Fans of port describe it as "a liquid symphony playing on the palate." Browse through the easy menu. Start white and sweet (cheapest), taste your way through spicy and ruby, and finish mellow and tawny. A *colheita* (single harvest) is particularly good. Appetizers *(aperitivos)* are listed in the menu with small photographs. As these are government employees and their jobs are secure, smiles or help navigating the menu are unnecessary. Table service can be slow and disinterested when it's busy; to be served without a long wait, go to the bar (Mon-Fri 11:00-24:00, Sat 14:00-24:00, closed Sun, directly across from the top of the Elevador da Glória funicular at Rua São Pedro de Alcântara 45). For more on port, see page 119.

Príncipe Real Garden Eateries (Jardim do Príncipe Real)

This delightful parklike square is just a five-minute hike up Rua Dom Pedro V above the top of the Elevador da Glória funicular and the Bairro Alto. While this area is becoming known as a shopping mecca (see under "Shopping in Lisbon," earlier), it also has a delightful array of eateries.

The park itself has an unforgettable cedar tree shaped into a canopy over shady benches and a *quiosque* that doubles as a trendy, youthful wine and beer hangout. Also below the tree's canopy is **$$$ Esplanada do Príncipe Real,** with delightful seating—either at outdoor tables under shady branches or in the glassed-in interior. Skip the pricey, forgettable food—I'd just order a drink and savor the ambience (tel. 210-965-699).

A block away (along Rua Dom Pedro V back toward the Bairro Alto) is the neighborhood's big foodie draw: **$$$ A Cevicheria,** where (under a giant stuffed octopus) Chef Kiko serves elegant Peruvian/Portuguese dishes—specializing in flavorfully marinated raw fish and seafood ceviche. This deservedly popular place takes no reservations; arrive early or expect to wait (daily 12:00-24:00, Rua Dom Pedro V 129, tel. 218-038-815, www.acevicheria.pt).

For a huge contrast, a few doors down is **$$ Pavilhão Chines** ("Chinese Pavilion")—an eccentric, smoky, private museum-like bar with room after room slathered with an enormous collection of esoteric treasures. Come here to settle into a club chair and sip a drink rather than to eat (daily from 18:00, Rua Dom Pedro V 89, billiards in back).

ON AVENIDA DA LIBERDADE

$$$$ Cervejaria Ribadouro is a favorite splurge for locals because of its quality meat and shellfish (daily 12:00-24:00, Avenida da Liberdade 155, at intersection with Rua do Salitre, M: Avenida, tel. 213-549-411). Seafood prices are listed by weight—the waiter can help you determine the cost of a portion. For a fun, quick, €14 per-person meal, order a small draught beer *(uma imperial)*, 100 grams (about a quarter-pound) of *percebes* (barnacles), and *pão torrado com manteiga* (toasted bread with butter).

$$$ Restaurante A Gina, glowing like a mirage in a vacant lot that used to be a theater zone, is one of my favorite places for a good dinner in Lisbon. It's a lunchtime hit with local office workers, who tuck in cloth bibs embroidered with Gina's name to appreciate the tasty traditional Portuguese grilled meat and fish. Gina and her staff scramble to give this wonderful place a genuine friendliness. Two minutes off of Avenida da Liberdade (directly behind recommended Hotel Lisboa Plaza—go between the white pillars and look left), it feels worlds away from the tourist crowds (daily 12:00-15:00 & 18:00-24:00, reservations recommended, tel. 213-420-296). The son, Rui, speaks English. Diners with this book get a free dessert port.

Lisbon Connections

BY PLANE

Lisbon's easy-to-manage Portela Airport is five miles northeast of downtown (airport code: LIS; for airport info, see www.aeroportolisboa.pt or call 218-413-700 or 800-201-201).

Getting Between the Airport and Downtown

Getting to and from the airport is a snap. Figure on 20 to 30 minutes by taxi, Uber, or bus (depending on traffic) or 30 to 40 minutes by Metro.

By Taxi or Uber: Taxis line up on the curb at the airport, but are notoriously aggressive in gouging arriving travelers. You're more likely to get a fair price—and skip any line—by going upstairs to the departures curb and hopping into a cab as it drops off its riders. Better yet, request a ride using Uber. Either way, a ride to or from town should cost no more than €10 to the center. If taking a taxi, insist on using the meter—it should start at around €4 and be set to *Tarifa 1* (or *Tarifa 2* for nights, weekends, and holidays). There is no "airport fee" supplement, but there is a legitimate €1.60 fee for your luggage (not per bag).

To return to the airport from downtown, simply use Uber or hail a cab on the street. Skip the outrageously overpriced "taxi vouchers" sold by the airport TI—these are for rides outside the center and more than double your cost.

By Bus: While dirt-cheap public buses leave from the airport curb, they are not intended for people with luggage. The Aerobus shuttle is faster and nearly as cheap (€3.50, 3/hour, runs 7:00-23:20, departs outside arrival level at bus stop marked "Aerobus #1," www.aerobus.pt). Be sure to use Aerobus #1, which heads to the city center, with stops at Marquês de Pombal, Avenida da Liberdade, Restauradores, Rossio, Praça do Comércio, and Cais do Sodré. Route #2 avoids the downtown and ends in the financial district, but makes a handy stop at the bus station at Sete Rios if you plan to go elsewhere immediately. Aerobus tickets are sold at the airport TI or on the bus for the same price. (But for three passengers, a taxi or Uber is likely cheaper than this bus.)

By Metro: The Metro gets you into town affordably (for the price of a single transit ticket) and avoids traffic. But to reach central Lisbon, you'll have to change from the airport's suburb-focused red line to the green line (at Alameda)—it's time-consuming (figure 30-40 minutes total) and inconvenient if you're packing heavy. To find the Metro, exit the airport arrivals hall and turn right to find the Aeroporto stop. Before boarding, buy a reloadable Viva Viagem card and your choice of ticket (zapping, single-ride, or all-day) at the ticket machine (see details under "Getting Around Lisbon" on page 10).

BY TRAIN

All of Lisbon's train stations are connected to the Metro system, making departures and arrivals a breeze. For train info, call 808-208-208, visit www.cp.pt, or check Germany's excellent all-Europe website, www.bahn.com.

Santa Apolónia station covers international trains and nearly all of Portugal. Located just east of the Alfama, it has ATMs, a morning-only TI, baggage storage, a Pingo Doce supermarket, and good Metro and bus connections to the town center. A taxi or Uber from Santa Apolónia to any of my recommended hotels costs roughly €8. Bus #728, #759, #782, and #794 go to or near Praça do Comércio, and bus #759 continues to Rossio and Praça dos Restauradores. To get to the bus stop from the station, look for the Metro sign, walk past the escalators to exit the station, and go right along busy Avenida Infante Dom Henrique to the bus stop.

Most trains using Santa Apolónia also stop at **Oriente** station, farther from the center, near Parque das Nações (M: Oriente; for more on this architecturally interesting station, see page 80).

Rossio station, which is in the town center and an easy walk from most recommended hotels, handles the most convenient trains to Sintra (direct, 2/hour, 40 minutes, buy tickets from machines at track level on second floor). It also has trains to Óbidos and Nazaré (but since both destinations require a transfer, the bus is a better option). The all-Portugal ticket office on the ground floor (next to Starbucks) sells long-distance and international train tickets (Mon-Fri 8:00-14:30 & 15:30-19:00, closed Sat-Sun, cash only).

Cais do Sodré station, near the waterfront just west of Praça do Comércio (M: Cais do Sodré), is the terminus for a short regional line that runs along the coast from Lisbon, making stops at Belém (10 minutes), Estoril (30 minutes), and Cascais (40 minutes).

Train Connections

Note: Any train leaving from Santa Apolónia passes through Oriente station a few minutes later.

From Lisbon by Train to: Madrid (1/day, "Lusitânia" night train, 11 hours, departs from Santa Apolónia station, arrives at

Madrid's Chamartín station), **Évora** (4/day, 1.5 hours, departs Oriente), **Lagos** (5/day, 4 hours, departs Oriente, transfer in Tunes or Faro), **Tavira** (5/day, 4-5 hours, departs Oriente, change at Faro), **Coimbra** (almost hourly, 2 hours, departs Santa Apolónia), **Nazaré/Valado** (3-5/day, 4 hours, involves 2-3 transfers; bus is better—see below), **Óbidos** (3/day, 2.5 hours, transfer in Sete Rios, departs Oriente; also 5/day, 2.5 hours, transfer in Mira Sintra-Melecas or Cacém, departs Rossio), **Porto** (almost hourly, 3 hours, departs Oriente), **Sintra** (2/hour, 40 minutes, departs Rossio; 4/hour, 50 minutes, departs Oriente).

To Salema: To reach Salema, you'll first need to get to **Lagos,** which is about 4 hours from Lisbon by train (see above) or bus (see next). Trains from Lisbon to the Algarve leave from Oriente station on the Lisboa-Faro line. At Tunes, a transfer to a local train takes you as far as Lagos. From there, it's a cheap bus ride or a pricier taxi ride to Salema.

BY BUS

Lisbon's efficient Sete Rios bus station is in the modern part of the city, three miles inland. It has ATMs, schedules, self-service info kiosks, and two information offices—one for buses within Portugal, the other for international routes (InterCentro Lines, which sells tickets for routes—including to Spain—even if operated by other companies). While it's possible to buy bus tickets up to a week in advance, you can almost always buy a ticket just a few minutes before departure. The EVA company covers the south of Portugal (www.eva-bus.com), while Rede Nacional de Expressos does the rest of the country (www.rede-expressos.pt; bus info for both companies—toll tel. 707-223-344).

The bus station is across the street from the large Sete Rios train station, which sits above the Jardim Zoológico Metro stop. To get from the bus station to downtown Lisbon, it's a €6 taxi or Uber ride or a short Metro trip on the blue line (from bus station, walk down and across to enter the Sete Rios train station, then follow signs for *Metro: Jardim Zoológico*).

From Lisbon by Bus to: Coimbra (hourly, 2.5 hours), **Nazaré** (6/day, 2 hours), **Fátima** (hourly, 1.5-2.5 hours), **Batalha** (5/day, 2 hours), **Alcobaça** (6/day, 2 hours, some transfer in Caldas da Rainha), **Óbidos** (hourly, 1 hour, departs from near Campo Grande Metro stop), **Porto** (at least hourly, 3 hours), **Évora** (almost hourly, 1.5 hours), **Lagos** (12 buses/day direct, 4 hours, easier than train, must book ahead, get details at TI), **Tavira** (5/day direct, 4.25 hours), **Madrid** (2-3/day, 8-9 hours, overnight option, www.avanzabus.com), **Sevilla** (2/day, 7 hours, overnight option, may be fewer off-season, run by Alsa, www.alsa.es).

BY CRUISE SHIP

Lisbon's port is the busiest on Europe's Atlantic coast, with most cruise ships docking at one of three terminals: Jardim do Tabaco (immediately below the Alfama), Santa Apolónia (near the train station of the same name, just beyond the Alfama), or Alcântara (about two miles west of downtown, between the center and Belém).

The taxis that wait at cruise terminals are notoriously dishonest. You may be better off using Uber, walking a block or two away from the terminal and hailing a passing cab on the street (not at a taxi stand), or riding a cruise-line shuttle service to Praça da Figueira. Hop-on, hop-off bus tours, which conveniently link up major sights—stop at the cruise terminals (see "Tours in Lisbon" earlier in this chapter).

From **Alcântara,** you can hop on trolley #15E (use pedestrian underpass to reach trolley stop) or bus #728—either way, it's about a 15-minute ride. (Both of these also go—in the opposite direction—to the sights in Belém.)

Jardim do Tobaco and **Santa Apolónia** are close enough to walk to the Baixa (15-20 minutes)—just go along busy Avenida Infante Dom Henrique with the river on your left, until you reach Praça do Comércio. Or you can take bus #728 from near either terminal to Praça do Comércio (at Santa Apolónia, the bus stop is in front of the train station, across the street).

SINTRA

For centuries, Portugal's aristocracy considered Sintra (SEEN-trah)—just 15 miles northwest of Lisbon—the perfect place to escape from city life. Now tourists do, too. Sintra is a mix of natural and manmade beauty: fantasy castles set amid exotic tropical plants, lush green valleys, and craggy hilltops with hazy views of the Atlantic and Lisbon. This was the summer getaway of Portugal's kings. Those with money and a desire to be close to royalty built their palaces amid luxuriant gardens in the same neighborhood. Lord Byron called this bundle of royal fancies and aristocratic dreams a "glorious Eden," and even though it's mobbed with tourists today, it's still magnificent.

With extra time, explore the rugged and picturesque westernmost tip of Portugal at Cabo da Roca.

PLANNING YOUR TIME

Sintra makes a great day trip from Lisbon. Here you can romp along the ruined ramparts of a deserted Moorish castle, and climb through the Versailles of Portugal—the Pena Palace—on a neighboring hilltop.

It's such an ideal side-trip, in fact, that Sintra can be miserably mobbed (especially July through Sept). Saturdays and Sundays are popular with Portuguese, while foreign tourists clog the town on Mondays (when many Lisbon museums are closed, but all major Sintra sights are open). Crowds are a bit lighter on Tuesdays through Fridays. Sintra's complicated landscape—with lots of hills and one-way roads between the big sights—adds to the challenge. A trip here requires patience and a flexible schedule. For the most stress-free visit possible, consider this good one-day plan:

Near Lisbon

Major Train Stations
1 Santa Apolónia
2 Oriente
3 Rossio
4 Cais do Sodré

Other
5 Belem to Porto
Brandão Ferry

Leave Lisbon around 8:30 to arrive in Sintra by 9:15 (most major sights open between 9:30 and 9:45—if you arrive much later, you'll be hopelessly mired in crowds all day). Pick up a map at the TI in Sintra's train station, and catch bus #434 in front of the station to Pena Palace. Visit the palace, walk down to the Moorish Castle ruins, scramble over its ramparts, then hike about 45 minutes back down to town via Vila Sassetti (or take bus #434). Have lunch (unless you already had a picnic, or lunched at the Pena Palace's café), explore the town, and—if you're not exhausted yet—visit the National Palace (right in town) or the Quinta da Regaleira (a 10-minute walk). Finally, catch the train back to Lisbon in time for dinner. This general plan also works well for drivers, who ideally should leave their car in Lisbon (or at least park in Sintra) and take advantage of public transportation.

Spending the night in Sintra is an intriguing option. This lets you get an earlier start, or visit the sights later in the day as crowds subside (the Moorish Castle is even better at closing time, with the sun low in the sky)—and also lets you savor the small town after dark, when it's quieter. Drivers in particular could consider overnighting in Sintra on the way to or from Lisbon.

GETTING TO SINTRA

Catch the **train** to Sintra from Lisbon's central Rossio station (direct, 2/hour, 40 minutes; also 4/hour from the less central Oriente station, 50 minutes). The trip is covered by the LisboaCard or the €10 version of Lisbon's all-day transit pass; if "zapping" with a Viva Viagem card, it's €2.15 each way (see page 10). Note that none of these passes work on local buses once you're in Sintra.

To avoid early-morning lines at the station in Lisbon, buy or charge up your card the night before (otherwise, buy it when you get to Rossio station—using the ticket machines or windows upstairs, at track level). During your ride, take in the views of the 18th-century aqueduct (on the left) and the workaday Lisbon suburbs. Relax...Sintra is at the end of the line.

Sintra is far easier by train than by **car** from Lisbon. Consider waiting until after you visit Sintra to pick up your rental car. If you do drive to Sintra, see "Route Tips for Drivers" on page 145.

Orientation to Sintra

Sintra is small. The town itself sprawls at the foot of a hill, an easy 10-minute walk (or quick bus ride) from the train station.

The National Palace, with its unmistakable pair of cone-shaped chimneys, is in the center of the town, a block from the TI, and the Quinta da Regaleira is a 10-minute walk away. But the other two main sights—Pena Palace and the Moorish Castle—hover on the hilltop above (you can see the castle's serrated wall on the hilltop). Most people take the bus up, but avid hikers enjoy the walk (figure an hour steeply uphill; see "Hiking Between Sintra and the Castles," later.)

TOURIST INFORMATION

Sintra has two TIs: a small one in the train station (daily 10:00-13:00 & 14:00-18:00, tel. 211-932-545) and a larger one a block off the main square in the Museu Regional building (daily 10:00-18:00, Aug until 19:00, tel. 219-231-157, www.askmelisboa.com). Pick up a free map with information on sights and a local Scotturb bus schedule. Hikers can download walking routes from the city website (www.cm-sintra.pt).

ARRIVAL IN SINTRA

By Train: Upon arrival, stop at the TI in the station. To **bus** to the town center, hop on Scotturb #434 (exit the station to the right to

reach the nearest stop, buy €5 all-day ticket from driver, schedules posted at stop; there's also a Scotturb office across the street from the station but it's extremely crowded in the morning; for more bus info, see "Getting Around Sintra," later). The bus stops in town first (at the National Palace, then near the main TI) before heading up to the Moorish Castle and Pena Palace, then loops back down to the station and town.

You can also reach the town center easily on **foot** (exit the station and go left, then turn left when you hit the turreted town hall)—it's about a 10-minute walk along a mostly level road along the lip of a ravine. Along the way you'll see modern "art" and hippies selling handmade trinkets.

By Car: See "Route Tips for Drivers" on page 145.

HELPFUL HINTS

Exchange Rate: €1 = about $1.10

Country Calling Code: 351 (see page 150 for dialing instructions)

LisboaCard: This sightseeing pass gets you discounts on the Pena Palace, Moorish Castle, National Palace, and the Monserrate gardens. It also covers the train ride from Lisbon to Sintra, but not the bus within Sintra (buy the LisboaCard at a Lisbon TI before you visit Sintra). Be sure to bring the LisboaCard booklet, which contains coupons required for some of the discounts.

Festivals: The lively Festival de Sintra music and dance festival runs from late May to early July (www.festivaldesintra.pt).

Money: You'll find a few ATMs near the train station, another inside the main TI, and one on Rua das Padarias, just up the hill from the recommended Casa Piriquita.

WCs: The only free WC in town—other than at restaurants—is located near the small, central parking lot where horse carriages wait (Calçada do Pelourinho).

Bring a Picnic: If saving a few euros is important, consider bringing a picnic from Lisbon—restaurants here can be pricey, though there is a very basic grocery store (see "Eating in Sintra," later).

Local Guide: Cristina Quental works mainly in Lisbon, but lives near Sintra and can meet you at the station (Mon-Fri €150/ half-day, €210/day; mobile 919-922-480, anacristinaquental@ hotmail.com).

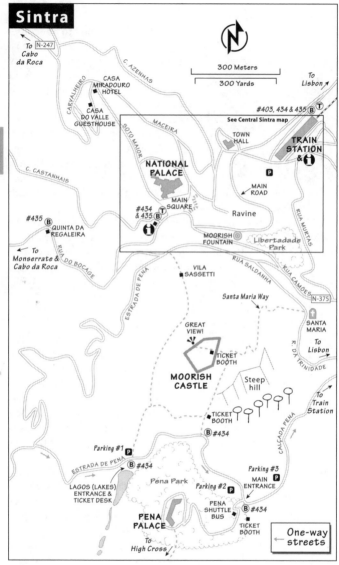

GETTING AROUND SINTRA

Whether you're driving, taking the bus, riding a taxi, or hopping in a tuk-tuk, you'll take the same very congested, single-lane, one-way road that loops up the hill and passes the main monuments. That means that no way is faster than any other—maybe just a bit more comfortable.

The best choice for most is **Scotturb Bus #434,** which loops together all the important stops—the train station, the town center (stops at the National Palace, then at the TI), the Moorish Castle ruins, and the Pena Palace—before heading back to town and the train station (4/hour—subject to traffic; €5 ticket good all day for one loop with stops, buy from driver or Scotturb staffer at stop near TI in town; first bus departs train station at 9:15; last bus leaves station at 19:50; entire circuit takes 30 minutes without traffic). A different bus, **#435,** goes from the train station to Quinta da Regaleira and the Monserrate gardens (1-3/hour, €2.50 one-way, also stops at TI, not covered by loop ticket).

Busy days bring very long lines at popular bus stops. Here are some **crowd-beating tips:** If there's a long line at the train station bus stop, consider walking into town and catching the bus at the National Palace instead. When returning to town from the Pena Palace, consider walking about 10 minutes (mostly downhill) back along the road to the Moorish Castle bus stop, where there's usually no line.

If the bus is a mob scene, you have alternatives. Noisy, bouncy, but fun **tuk-tuks** are all over Sintra, charging €5 per person for a breezy ride from town or the station to the Moorish Castle, Pena Palace, or Quinta da Regaleira (you can also book tuk-tuks for a "guided tour" loop). Or figure €10 for a **taxi** from the center up to any one of the sights.

Clip-clop **horse carriages** cost about €30 for 25 minutes. They can take you anywhere; you'll likely see them waiting on the little square near the bus stop just in front of the National Palace.

Sights in Sintra

Combo-tickets are available for the Pena Palace, Moorish Castle, and National Palace, but savings are minimal (about 5 percent)—ask when you buy your first ticket. Unless you're 100 percent certain you'll make it to all three sights, the combo deal is probably not worthwhile.

ON THE HILL ABOVE SINTRA

These sights cap the hill high above Sintra—connected by bus #434. If walking between them, figure 10 minutes between the Pena Palace main entrance and the Moorish Castle, and another 10 minutes to the Pena Palace's lower "Lakes/Lagos" entrance. Be careful walking along the congested road, with its narrow shoulder and ankle-twisting cobbles.

▲▲Pena Palace (Palácio de Pena)

This magical hilltop palace sits high above Sintra, above the Moorish Castle ruins. In the 19th century, Portugal had a very romantic prince, the German-born Prince Ferdinand. A contemporary and cousin of Bavaria's "Mad" King Ludwig (of Disneyesque Neuschwanstein Castle fame), Ferdinand was also a cousin of England's Prince Albert (Queen Victoria's husband). Flamboyant Ferdinand hired a German architect to build a fantasy castle, mixing elements of German and Portuguese style.

He ended up with a crazy Neo-fortified casserole of Gothic towers, Renaissance domes, Moorish minarets, Manueline carvings, Disneyland playfulness, and an *azulejo* (tile) toilet for his wife.

Cost and Hours: Palace and gardens—€14, shuttle bus—€3 round-trip (buy with your palace ticket); daily May-mid-Sept 9:30-19:00, last entry 45 minutes before closing, gardens stay open an hour after palace closing time, shorter hours off-season; tel. 219-105-340, www.parquesdesintra.pt.

Getting In: There are two entrances to the castle grounds: the lower "Lakes/Lagos" entrance (at the bottom of the park, across from the first parking lot you come to), and the main entrance (just below the castle itself). It's a 20-minute walk between these two (you'll pass the Moorish Castle ticket booth between them). While the lower entrance is less crowded, it's best to use the main entrance if possible, since it's closer to the castle.

At the main entrance, purchase your ticket at the small hut next to the gate (if there's a long line, look for ticket machines just downhill—toward the Moorish Castle). To avoid the 15-minute uphill climb from the entrance to the palace (and enjoy a lift back down later), catch the green shuttle bus, which departs from straight ahead as you enter (€3 round-trip, buy with your palace ticket—or inside gift shop—but *not* from driver, departs about every 10 minutes).

Eating: The palace has an inexpensive **$** view café and a pricier **$$** restaurant. If you brought your lunch with you, enjoy it in the picnic-perfect gardens either before or after your visit—with views fit for a king.

◑ Self-Guided Tour: English descriptions throughout the palace give meaning to the rooms. Be sure to pick up the *Parques e Palácios* map, with a helpful illustration of the castle on one side and a circular, 1.5-hour walking route of the park on the other. For even more info, rent the €3 audioguide.

The palace, built in the mid- to late-1800s, is so well-preserved that it feels as if it's the day after the royal family fled Portugal in 1910 (during a popular revolt that eventually made way for today's modern republic). This gives the place a charming intimacy rarely seen in palaces. Here are the highlights.

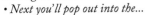

• *After you hop off the green shuttle bus, hike up the ramp and show your ticket at the Moorish archway with alligator decor. Cross the drawbridge that doesn't draw, and join a slack-jawed world of tourists frozen in deep knee-bends with their cameras cocked.*

Palace Interior: Show your ticket again to enter the palace itself. Inside, at the base of the stairs, you'll see King Ferdinand, who built this castle from 1840 until his death in 1885. Though German, he was a romantic proponent of his adopted culture and did much to preserve Portugal's architectural and artistic heritage.

• *Next you'll pop out into the...*

Courtyard: The palace was built on the site of a 16th-century monastery; the courtyard was the former location of the cloister. In spite of its plushness, the palace retains the monkish coziness of several small rooms gathered in two levels around the cloister.

Like its big brother in Belém, the monastery housed followers of St. Jerome, the hermit monk. Like their namesake, the monks wanted to be isolated, and this was about as isolated as you could be around here 500 years ago. The spot was also a popular pilgrimage destination for its statue of "Our Lady of the Feathers" (*pena* means feather—hence the palace's name). In 1498 King Manuel was up here enjoying the view when he spied Vasco da Gama sailing up the river, returning safely from his great voyage. To celebrate and give thanks, the king turned what was a humble wooden monastery into a fine stone palace.

• *From here, follow the one-way route counterclockwise around the courtyard, dipping into a variety of rooms. These are especially worthy of attention.*

Dining Room and Pantry: Stuck into a cozy corner, the monastery's original refectory was decked out with the royal family's finest tableware and ceiling tiles.

Atelier (Workshop) of King Carlos I: With a shaky empire crumbling around him, King Carlos found refuge in art—specifically the latest style, Art Nouveau. Unfinished paintings and sketches eerily predict the king's unfinished rule.

SINTRA

King's Bedroom and Bathroom: The king enjoyed cutting-edge comforts, including a shower/tub imported from England, and even a telephone to listen to the opera when he couldn't face the Lisbon commute. The bedroom is decorated in classic Romantic style—dark, heavy, and crowded with knickknacks.

• *Now head upstairs (gripping the funky dragon-like handrail). Circling around the courtyard, you'll enter the wing called the Piano Nobile ("noble floor"). Go through a few daintily decorated rooms that belonged to ladies-in-waiting, and then enter the...*

Queen's Bedroom and Dressing Room: Study the melancholy photos of Queen Amelia (Amélie of Orléans), King Carlos, and their family in this room. The early 1900s were a rocky time for Portugal's royal family. The king and his eldest son were assassinated in 1908. His youngest son, Manuel II, became king until he, his mother the queen, and other members of the royal family fled Portugal during the 1910 revolution.

As you shuffle through the palace, you'll see state-of-the-art conveniences—such as the first flush toilets and hot shower in Portugal, and even a telephone room. The whole place is lovingly cluttered, typical of the Victorian horror of empty spaces.

• *At the end of this floor, step out onto the...*

Queen's Terrace: Enjoy a sweeping view from Lisbon to the mouth of the Rio Tejo. Find the Cristo Rei statue and the 25th of April Bridge. The statue on the distant ridge honors the palace's architect.

• *Heading back inside, you'll pass through some smaller rooms, then enter...*

The New Wing: This spacious addition to the original series of rooms around the cloister includes the apartments of the last king, the smoking room (with a tiled ceiling), and the fantastically furnished Great Hall.

On your way down the spiral staircase, take a detour to see the **Stag Room**—with well-antlered walls and a dramatic dome supported by a stout, palm-tree-like column. From here, you'll head down to see the abundant kitchen.

Just after, a view café conveniently welcomes us peasants. While many people take this as a sign to leave, we haven't yet seen some of the most scenic parts of the castle.

• *From the café, turn left and walk alongside the palace, then duck through one of the two huge, ornamental gateways on your left (the second one has a scowling Triton overhead). You'll emerge into the...*

Inner Patio: Take the stairs up to the pointed dome covered in green and white tiles (in front of the tallest red tower). This was the royal family's sumptuous private **chapel,** decorated in a variety of styles. The structure is Manueline, reminiscent of the Monastery of Jerónimos in Belém.

• *Heading back down into the patio, don't miss the little door under the chapel marked...*

The Wall Walk: Follow this for a rampart ramble with great views—of the onion-domed balustrade, of the palace itself, and of the surrounding countryside—including the Moorish Castle on an adjacent hilltop. You'll circle all the way around the outside of the palace, and wind up back at the entrance.

• *From here, you can return directly to the main entrance (walk 10 minutes or catch the green shuttle bus—your ticket covers the round-trip), or detour for a self-guided tour of the park.*

Pena Palace Park: The lush, captivating, and sprawling palace grounds—rated ▲—are dotted with romantic surprises. Several landmarks within the park are signposted near the shuttle bus stop. Highlights include the High Cross (highest point around, with commanding views), chapels, a temple, lakes, giant sequoia trees, and exotic plants. To walk through the park after you tour the palace, take a 40-minute stroll downhill (following the map that came with your palace entry) to the lower park gate, at the Lakes/Lagos entry, where you'll find a bus stop and the Estrada de Pena loop road. From here, it's a ten-minute hike uphill to the Moorish Castle, or a 20-minute hike back to the Pena Palace's main entrance.

▲Moorish Castle (Castelo dos Mouros)

Sintra's thousand-year-old ruins of a Moorish castle are lost in an enchanted forest and alive with winds of the past. They're a castle lover's dream come true, and a great place for a picnic with a panoramic Atlantic view. Though built by the Moors, the castle was taken by Christian forces in 1147. It's one of the most classically perfect castles you'll find anywhere, with two hills capped by hardy forts, connected by a crenellated wall walkway. (It's so idealized because it was significantly restored in the 19th century.)

Cost and Hours: €8, daily 9:30-20:00, last entry one hour before closing, tel. 219-237-300, www.parquesdesintra.pt.

Getting In: From the main ticket booth (near the bus stop) to the castle entrance, it's an atmospheric 10-minute stroll—mostly downhill—through a forested canyon, passing a few small exhibits and information plaques. If the main ticket booth is crowded, bypass it and simply continue to the castle itself, where there's another ticket booth that rarely has a wait. Either way, be sure to pick up the well-illustrated map, which has lots of insightful information.

Visiting the Castle: You'll enter the castle in a terraced area with a cafeteria, shop, and WCs, all sitting on top of a cistern. The castle walls and towers climb hills on either side of you. Do a hardy counterclockwise hike, conquering the lower one first, then heading up to the higher one.

From where you entered, go right and take the stony stairs up to the keep. From the top tower, you can see how the wall twists and turns—following the contours of the land—as it connects over to the taller hilltop tower. Follow the crenellated path, with delirious views over Sintra down below and as far as the Atlantic. You'll go down, then back up the other side, ascending higher and higher to the top of the Royal Tower. From the summit, you enjoy great views across to Pena Palace, perched on its adjacent hilltop. From this pinnacle, you can gingerly descend to the cafeteria and entrance—having conquered the castle.

Hiking Between Sintra and the Castles

It's a steep one-hour hike from town up to the Moorish Castle and Pena Palace—challenging even for hardy hikers. But hiking back down to town after your hilltop visits (rather than cramming into an overstuffed bus) is an appealing 45-minute possibility for those with strong knees. Be sure to equip yourself with the TI's invaluable *Pedestrian Route* map—and get their advice—before you set out (maps may also be available at Moorish Castle or Pena Palace ticket offices).

The best route is to take a terraced path directly below the Moorish Castle, which leads past the **Vila Sassetti.** You'll find the trailhead at the end of the parking lot directly across from the Lakes/Lagos lower entrance of the Pena Palace grounds, and you'll also find a trail connecting to it near the Moorish Castle main ticket booth (near the bus stop). From here, the trail curls around the bottom of the Moorish Castle's rocky perch, then enters the grounds of the Vila Sassetti (open daily 10:00-18:00, or until 17:00 off-season). Designed by theater set decorator Luigi Manini (who also did the Quinta da Regaleira, described later), the Vila Sassetti looks like an old Roman house with a terra cotta roof. You'll hike down to the villa itself, then traipse through its lower gardens into Sintra. (If the Villa is closed, you can also drop down—on steep steps—to footpaths that run through the woods above the main road.)

Yet another option is to walk down on the **"Santa Maria Way,"** which forks off in the opposite direction from the Moorish Castle entrance. However, this trail is mostly through thick woods and less scenic.

IN TOWN
These sights are all within easy walking distance of the town center.

▲National Palace (Palácio Nacional)
While the palace dates back to Moorish times, most of what you'll see is from the 15th-century reign of King João I, with later Manueline architectural ornamentation from the 16th century. This oldest surviving royal palace in Portugal is still used for official receptions. Having housed royalty for 500 years (until 1910), it's fragrant with history.

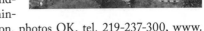

Cost and Hours: €10, daily 9:30-19:00; look for white, double-coned building in town center, 10-minute walk from train station, photos OK, tel. 219-237-300, www.parquesdesintra.pt.

 ➲ **Self-Guided Tour:** The palace is a one-way romp with little information provided. The €3 audioguide is informative, but as dry as an Alentejo summer; free English tours depart the entrance at 14:30. If touring on your own, read the brief descriptions in each room, and tune into the following notable parts of the palace.

• *Show your ticket, then head upstairs into...*

Swan Room: This first room is the palace's banquet room. A king's daughter—who loved swans—married into a royal house in Belgium. The king missed the princess so much that he decorated the ceiling with her favorite animal. These aren't the only creatures in the room, though. Check out the ceramic soup tureens designed in the shape of your favorite barnyard animal.

Central Patio: This was a fortified medieval palace, so rather than having fancy gardens outside, it has a stay-awhile courtyard within its protective walls. Notice the unique chimneys. They provide powerful suction that removes the smoke from the kitchen and also create a marvelous open-domed feeling (as you'll see at the end of your tour).

Magpie Room: The queen caught King João I being a little too friendly with a lady-in-waiting. Frustrated by his court—abuzz with gossip—João had this ceiling painted with magpies. But to defend his honor, he illustrated each magpie quoting the king's slogan—*Por bem,* "For good." The 15th-century Moorish tiles are from Spain, brought in before the development of the famous, ubiquitous Portuguese tiles, and are considered some of the finest Moorish-Spanish tiles in all of Iberia.

Bedchamber of King Sebastian (Dom Sebastião): The king portrayed on the wall (to the right of where you enter) is King Sebastian, a gung-ho, medieval-type monarch who went to battle in Africa, following the Moors even after they were chased out of Europe. He disappeared in 1578 at age 24 (although he was almost certainly killed in Morocco, "Sebastianists" awaited his mythical return into the 19th century). With the king missing, Portugal was left in unstable times with only Sebastian's great uncle (King Henrique) as heir. The new king died within two years, and the throne passed to his great uncle, King Philip II of Spain, leading to 60 years of Spanish rule (1580-1640).

Note the ebony, silver, and painted copper headboard of the Italian Renaissance bed. The tiles in this room are considered the first Portuguese tiles—from the time of Manuel I. The corn-on-the-cob motif topping the tilework is a reminder of American discoveries.

More Main-Floor Rooms: From here, you'll walk through the **Julius Caesar Room,** with a Flemish tapestry of the Roman general-turned-ruler; the **Goddess Diana Courtyard;** and up the stairs to the **Galleon Room,** whose ceiling is painted with ships flying the flags of the great nautical powers of the day. Step out onto the balcony for views of a forested hillside scattered with the villas of aristocrats—and capped by the serrated wall of the Moorish Castle. Then, head up the stairs to walk through some smaller, simpler apartments with a few original furnishings.

• *Finally, you step into the glorious...*

Blazons Hall (a.k.a. Coat of Arms Room): The most striking room in the palace—under a golden dome and slathered in blue tiles—honors Portugal's loyal nobility. Study the richly decorated ceiling. The king's coat of arms at the top is surrounded by the coats of arms of his children; below that is a ring of stags; and finally, at the bottom, are the coats of arms of all but one of Portugal's noble families (the omitted family had schemed a revolt, so received only a blank niche). The Latin phrase circling the room reads, "Honoring all the noble families who've been loyal to the king." The 18th-century tiles hang from the walls like tapestries. Enjoy the view: a garden-like countryside dotted with mansions of nobility who clamored to be near their king, the hill-capping castle, and the wide-open Atlantic. You're in

the westernmost room of the westernmost palace on the European continent.

• *Continue through the upper halls, peeking into the...*

Bedchamber and Prison of Alfonso VI: This king suffered

from a fever as a child that left him mentally unstable. After he became king, he was removed by his wife and his brother—who became King Pedro II, locked him in this room for the rest of his life, and married his queen.

Yet More Rooms: As you continue, you'll pass through the **Chinese Room** (with an exquisite ivory-and-bone model of a Chinese pagoda). Downstairs, you can step out onto a private balcony and peer down into the **Palatine Chapel,** with a Mudejar wood-carved ceiling. Then you'll pass through a room of coffers (literal treasure chests) and head downstairs to the **Arab Room**—decorated with Moorish tiles, and with a little fountain in the middle; this was the preferred bedroom of João I. From here, you'll walk through a fancy **guest room** and into the **kitchen.** With all the latest in cooking technology, the palace chef could roast an entire cow on the spit, keep the king's plates warm in the iron dish warmer (with drawers below for the charcoal), and get really dizzy by looking up and spinning around three times.

On your way out, as you step back into the big entry hall, be sure to detour left into the **Manueline Room,** with carved-stone ropes over the doors and a grand chandelier, and a handy WC in the corner. You'll walk back through the Central Patio (peek into the blue-tiled **Grotto of the Baths** in the corner) and head for the exit. On your way out, watch for the easy-to-miss door on the right that lets you explore the manicured, terraced **gardens** surrounding the palace.

SOUTHWEST OF THE CENTER

These two sights line up on a road southwest of central Sintra. You can walk to Quinta da Regaleira, but Monserrate is quite a bit farther. Bus #435 stops at each one (see details earlier, under "Getting Around Sintra"), or you can take a tuk-tuk or taxi.

▲▲Quinta da Regaleira

This Neo-Everything (Manueline/ Gothic/Renaissance) 1912 mansion and garden has mystical and Masonic twists. It was designed by Italian opera-set designer Luigi Manini for a wealthy but disgruntled monarchist two years after the royal family was deposed. While the mansion—prickly with spires—is striking from the outside, its interior is nothing compared to the Pena Palace or National Palace. But the grounds are an utter delight to wander, with fanciful follies, secret

SINTRA

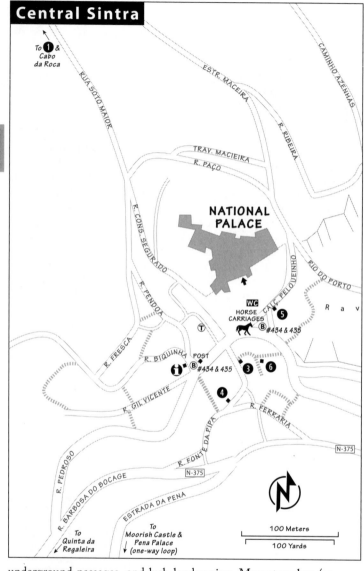

Central Sintra

To ❶ & Cabo da Roca

RUA SOTO MAIOR

ESTR. MACEIRA

CAMINHO AZENHAS

TRAV. MACIEIRA

R. PAÇO

R. RIBEIRA

R. CONS. SEGURADO

NATIONAL PALACE

R. PENDOA

RIO DO PORTO

CALÇ. PELOUEINHO

R a v

WC

HORSE CARRIAGES

❺

Ⓑ #434 & 435

Ⓣ

R. FRESCA

R. BIQUINHA

POST

❶ Ⓑ #434 & 435

❸ ❻

R. GIL VICENTE

❹

R. FERRARIA

N-375

R. PEDROSO

R. BARBOSA DO BOCAGE

R. FONTE DA PIPA

N-375

ESTRADA DA PENA

To Quinta da Regaleira

To Moorish Castle & Pena Palace (one-way loop)

100 Meters

100 Yards

underground passages, and lush landscaping. Many travelers (especially younger ones) find romping around these grounds more enjoyable than shuffling around the crowded interiors of the more famous palaces. Ask a local to pronounce "Regaleira" for you, and just try to repeat it.

Cost and Hours: €6, daily 10:00-20:00, closes earlier off-season, last entry one hour before closing, 10-minute walk from downtown Sintra, café, tel. 219-106-650, www.regaleira.pt.

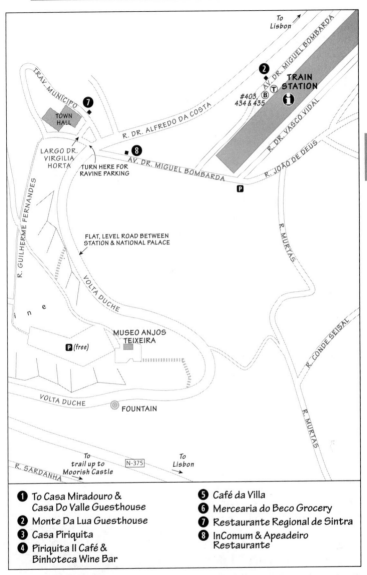

① To Casa Miradouro &
   Casa Do Valle Guesthouse
② Monte Da Lua Guesthouse
③ Casa Piriquita
④ Piriquita II Café &
   Binhoteca Wine Bar
⑤ Café da Villa
⑥ Mercearia do Beco Grocery
⑦ Restaurante Regional de Sintra
⑧ InComum & Apeadeiro
   Restaurante

Tours: Excellent two-hour English tours fill up, so book ahead online or by phone (€10, includes entry, about hourly April-Sept, fewer off-season). The tour focuses on the garden, but can be longish unless you're into quirky Masonic esoterica.

Visiting the Quinta: As you enter, be sure to pick up the superb illustrated map of both the house and the gardens.

The **mansion** itself is striking—as it was designed to be. (In fact, that was its sole purpose.) You'll enter through the finest space, the Hunting Room, with an outrageously carved fireplace. From here you can explore three floors, filled mostly with well-presented exhibits on the design and construction of the place, and biographical sketches of the aristocrat and the architect who brought it to life. At the top floor, find the tight spiral stone staircase up to the view terrace.

The real highlight is the playful **gardens,** which stretch uphill from the mansion. Work your way up, past the elaborate private chapel, then to higher and higher crenellated viewpoints. Follow *Waterfall* signs to reach a refreshing artificial canyon with ponds and a cascade. Stepping stones lead across the main pond to the grottos that hide beneath, giving you a unique perspective. From the top of the waterfall, continue up to the "Portal of the Guardians"; inside, secret tunnels lead to the dramatic, spiral-staircase-wrapped well—burrowed 90 feet down into the hillside, and, like the rest of Quinta da Regaleira, more about showing off than about being functional. From here, more tunnels lead to other parts of the property; use your map to explore to your heart's content.

Monserrate

About 2.5 miles outside of Sintra—on the road past the Quinta da Regaleira—are the wonderful gardens of Monserrate. If you like tropical plants and exotic landscaping, a visit is time well-spent, though many find that the gardens at Pena Palace or the Quinta da Regaleira are just as good as these more famous grounds.

Cost and Hours: €8, park open daily 9:30-20:00, palace open until 19:00, last ticket sold for each one hour before closing, tel. 219-237-300, www.parquesdesintra.pt.

WEST OF SINTRA, ON THE COAST
Cabo da Roca

Wind-beaten, tourist-infested Cabo da Roca (KAH-boo dah ROH-kah) is the westernmost point in Europe, perhaps the inspiration for the Portuguese poet Luís de Camões' line, *"Onde a terra se acaba e o mar começa"* ("Where land ends and the sea begins"). It has a little shop, a café, and a tiny TI that sells an expensive "proof of being here" certificate. Take a photo instead (tel. 219-280-801). Nearby, on the road south to Cascais, you'll pass a good beach for wind, waves, sand, and the chance to  be the last person in Europe to see the sun set. For a remote beach, drive to Praia Adraga (north of Cabo da Roca).

SINTRA

Sleep Code

Hotels are classified based on the average price of a standard double room with breakfast in high season.

$$$$	**Splurge:** Most rooms over €150
$$$	**Pricier:** €100-150
$$	**Moderate:** €70-100
$	**Budget:** €40-70
¢	**Backpacker:** Under €40
RS%	**Rick Steves discount**

Unless otherwise noted, credit cards are accepted, hotel staff speaks basic English, and free Wi-Fi is available. Comparison-shop by checking prices at several hotels (on each hotel's own website, on a booking site, or by email). For the best deal, *book directly with the hotel*. Ask for a discount if paying in cash; if the listing includes **RS%**, request a Rick Steves discount.

Sleeping in Sintra

Sintra works well as an overnight—allowing you to beat the crowds by tackling the sights early or late, and having the charming town to yourself after hours. To reach the first two places, you'll head into town, turn right to pass in front of the National Palace, then continue steeply downhill on the road past Hotel Tivoli; they face each other at the very bottom of the street (free street parking, steep 10-minute hike back up to the town center). The final listing—cheaper and handier for train travelers—is directly across the street from the train station.

$$$ Casa Miradouro is a beautifully restored mansion from 1893, now run by Belgian expat Charlotte Lambregts. The creaky old house feels like a homey, upscale British B&B, with eight spacious, stylish rooms, an elegant lounge, castle and sea views, and a wonderful garden (good breakfast extra, Rua Sotto Major 55, mobile 914-292-203, www.casa-miradouro.com, mail@casa-miradouro.com).

$$ Casa Do Valle Guesthouse offers 11 comfortable, modern rooms on several levels in a peaceful hillside location. They have a lovely garden and large deck with valley and castle views, a swimming pool, and a shared kitchen (extra for continental breakfast in your room, reception open until 18:30, behind Casa Miradouro at Rua da Paderna 5, tel. 219-244-699, www.casadovalle.com, info@casadovalle.com).

$ Monte Da Lua Guesthouse has seven clean, simple rooms with shiny hardwood floors; some rooms face the train station, while others face a quieter ravine in the back (cheaper rooms with shared bath, no breakfast, Avenida Dr. Miguel Bombarda 51, tel. 210-129-659, www.montedalua.net, montedalua51@gmail.com).

Eating in Sintra

All of these listings are in the town of Sintra. To eat at the hilltop sights, there are cafés at both Pena Palace and the Moorish Palace, or you can pack a picnic.

LIGHT MEALS

Most of these (except Café da Villa) are on or near Rua das Padarias, the touristy little cobbled lane across the street from the National Palace. The sit-down restaurants in this zone are very pricey and touristy, but these are handy for a light, quick meal.

$ Casa Piriquita bills itself as "the" *antiga fabrica de queijadas*—historic maker of tiny, tasty tarts with a cheesy filling. It's good for a sweet and a coffee or a simple lunch, such as toasted sandwiches. Take a seat in the café (up a few steps) to avoid groups who rush in to get pastries to go, or do battle and grab a half-dozen for about €5 (Tue-Thu 8:30-22:00, closed Wed, Rua das Padarias 1, tel. 219-230-626).

$ Piriquita II, sister to Casa Piriquita, is a block farther up the lane and may have less commotion. It has a more extensive menu and a view terrace (Wed-Mon 8:30-20:00, closed Tue, Rua das Padarias 18).

$$ Binhoteca, a welcoming little *enoteca,* provides wine lovers with an astonishing array of Portuguese wines and ports available by the glass (starting at €5), along with tasty meat-and-cheese plates, sandwiches, and salads. The knowledgeable staff is happy to explain what you're enjoying. It's a fun experience, but prices can add up (daily 10:00-19:00—and often later, Rua das Padarias 16, tel. 219-230-444).

$$ Café da Villa, a favorite of bus drivers and tour guides, offers generous portions of homemade-style soups and salads in a homey pub-like setting. It's good for a quiet, inexpensive lunch, with a variety of fixed-price meal options (daily 12:00-24:00, facing the little bus-stop square in front of the National Palace at Calçada do Pelourinho 2, tel. 219-241-174).

Groceries: Mercearia do Beco, just a few steps off Rua das Padarias, is a basic grocery store where you can assemble a picnic (daily 9:00-22:00, Rua Arco do Teixeira 17).

DINING

While there are plenty of tourist eateries in Sintra's old center, for a serious meal I'd head a couple of blocks away to the station area.

$$ Restaurante Regional de Sintra, which feeds locals and

Restaurant Price Code

I've assigned each eatery a price category, based on the aver-age cost of a typical main course. Drinks, desserts, and splurge items (steak and seafood) can raise the price considerably.

$$$$	**Splurge:** Most main courses over €17
$$$	**Pricier:** €12-17
$$	**Moderate:** €7-12
$	**Budget:** Under €7

In Portugal, takeout food is **$**; a basic sit-down eatery is **$$**; a casual but more upscale restaurant is **$$$**; and a swanky splurge is **$$$$**.

---

tourists very well, is my favorite place for dinner in Sintra. Gentle Paulo speaks English and serves huge, splittable portions (Tue-Thu 12:00-16:00 & 19:00-22:30, closed Wed, tucked to the right of the turreted town hall at Travessa do Municipio 2, tel. 219-234-444).

$$$ InComum is working hard to bring a modern sensi-bility to traditional Portuguese cooking. The owners, who lived in Switzerland, pride themselves on serving Portuguese-inspired dishes with updated, international flair. The minimalist dining room is especially popular at lunchtime, when the weekday lunch special offers an affordable taste of their cooking (daily 12:00-24:00, Rua Dr. Alfredo Coasta 22, tel. 219-243-719, www.incomumbyluissantos.pt).

$$ Apeadeiro Restaurante, named for the platform along the track at the train station just a block away, is a quality eatery serving good food at good prices. Their daily specials can be split, allowing two to eat affordably (Fri-Wed 9:00-24:00, closed Thu, Avenida Dr. Miguel Bombarda 3, tel. 219-231-804).

Sintra Connections

From Sintra by Train and Bus to: Lisbon (2 trains/hour to Ros-sio station, 40 minutes; 4 trains/hour to Oriente station, 50 min-utes), **Cascais** (bus #403 via Cabo da Roca, 45-60 minutes, 1-2/hour; express bus #417, 30 minutes, hourly; both buses fewer on weekends, catch either one at the Sintra train station).

ROUTE TIPS
Sintra Day Trip from Lisbon by Car

Cars are the curse of Sintra—all traffic, from cars to buses to tuk-tuks, has to nudge through town on a two-lane road, and parking is difficult (especially up at the hilltop castles).

If you insist on taking a car to Sintra, take the IC-19 freeway out of Lisbon (allow 30 minutes, not counting traffic delays). When you arrive in Sintra, follow *Centro Histórico* signs. It's probably smartest to simply park your car and use bus #434 to get around. The road into town (Volta do Duche) has some pay-and-display parking—see what you can find (4-hour maximum). And there's free parking on the road just behind the train station.

If you anticipate crowds and don't want to hunt for a space, park in the (relatively) large lot down in the ravine between the train station and the TI. As you come into town, watch for the colorful, turreted town hall building on your right; take the tiny lane immediately after that building (the *no entry* signs are just for campers) and head down to the lot next to the Museu Anjos Teixeira. Climb up the stairs next to the museum, and you're on the main road into town.

It's tempting to drive up the **Moorish Castle** and **Pena Palace,** but be warned that parking up top is very limited and fills up fast (often jammed already by about 10:00 on busy days). The road makes a very long, one-way loop with no backtracking, so if you don't find a space you'll have to complete the loop and return back to the center. But if you're feeling lucky, here's the plan: Head up the road with every other car and bus in town. You'll twist up, up, up on a dozen switchbacks. Approaching the sights, there are three marked parking lots (one by the lower Lakes/Lagos entrance to Pena Palace; another just before the main entrance to Pena Palace—this is probably your most convenient choice, if it has space; and a third one, just past the main entrance to Pena Palace). Monitors along the road suggest which lots might have space, and which are *completo*. All along the congested, cobbled road are a few well-marked roadside spaces. It's best to park as soon as you find something—anything—and then walk the rest of the way to connect the sights.

It's possible to make a **70-mile circular trip** and drive to all the destinations near Lisbon within a day (Lisbon–Belém–Sintra–Cabo da Roca–Cascais–Lisbon), but traffic congestion around Sintra, especially on weekends and during rush hour, can slow you down.

Loop Trip by Public Transportation

If you're bent on seeing sights west of Lisbon—Sintra, Cabo da Roca, and Cascais—in a single long day, it can be done using public transportation. Start at the Sintra train station and buy a day pass for the Scotturb **bus** (€12). Use the pass to take bus #434 to Sintra's sights, then go to Cabo da Roca on bus #403. When you're ready, catch the next bus #403 for the jaunt to Cascais and a seafood dinner on the waterfront (for more on Cascais, see page 101). If you want to head from Sintra straight to Cascais—without the Cabo da Roca detour—take the faster bus #417.

From Cascais, returning to Lisbon is a snap—just buy a one-way **train** ticket to Lisbon at the train station. You'll get off at the last stop on the line (Cais de Sodré Station), a five-minute walk from Praça do Comércio in downtown Lisbon. Or, to return to Sintra, hop on bus #417.

PRACTICALITIES

This section covers just the basics on traveling in Portugal (for much more information, see *Rick Steves Portugal*). You'll find free advice on specific topics at www.ricksteves.com/tips.

Money

Portugal uses the euro currency: 1 euro (€) = about $1.10. To convert prices in euros to dollars, add about 10 percent: €20 = about $22, €50 = about $55. (Check www.oanda.com for the latest exchange rates.)

The standard way for travelers to get euros is to withdraw money from an ATM (known as a *Multibanco* in Portugal—look for the *MB* logo) using a debit or credit card. Before departing, call your bank or credit-card company: Confirm that your card(s) will work overseas, ask about international transaction fees, and alert them that you'll be making withdrawals in Europe. Note that in Portugal, the maximum you can withdraw per transaction is €200.

Also ask for the PIN number for your credit card—you may need it for Europe's "chip-and-PIN" payment machines (see below; allow time for your bank to mail your PIN to you). To keep your valuables safe, wear a money belt.

Dealing with "Chip and PIN": Newer credit and debit cards have chips that authenticate and secure transactions. In Europe, the cardholder inserts the chip card into the payment machine slot, then enters a PIN. (In the US, you provide a signature.) Any American card, whether with a chip or an old-fashioned magnetic stripe, will work at Europe's hotels, restaurants, and shops. But some self-service chip-and-PIN payment machines—such as those at train stations, toll roads, or unattended gas pumps—may not accept your card. If your card won't work, look for a cashier who can process the transaction manually—or pay in cash.

Dynamic Currency Conversion: If merchants or hoteliers offer to convert your purchase price into dollars (called dynamic currency conversion, or DCC), refuse this "service." You'll pay extra for the expensive convenience of seeing your charge in dollars. If an ATM offers to "lock in" or "guarantee" your conversion rate, choose "proceed without conversion." Other prompts might state, "You can be charged in dollars: Press YES for dollars, NO for euros." Always choose the local currency.

Staying Connected

The simplest solution is to bring your own device—mobile phone, tablet, or laptop—and use it just as you would at home (following the tips below, such as connecting to free Wi-Fi whenever possible).

To call Portugal from a US or Canadian number: Whether you're phoning from a landline, your own mobile phone, or a Skype account, you're making an international call. Dial 011-351 and then the local number. (011 is our international access code; 351 is Portugal's country code.) If dialing from a mobile phone, you can enter + in place of the international access code—press and hold the 0 key.

To call Portugal from a European country: Dial 00-351 followed by the local number. (00 is Europe's international access code.)

To call within Portugal: Just dial the local number.

To call from Portugal to another country: Dial 00 followed by the country code (for example, 1 for the US or Canada), then the area code and number. If you're calling European countries whose phone numbers begin with 0, you'll usually have to omit that 0 when you dial.

Tips: If you bring your own mobile phone, consider getting an international plan; most providers offer a global calling plan that cuts the per-minute cost of phone calls and texts, and a flat-fee data plan.

Use Wi-Fi whenever possible. Most hotels and many cafés offer free Wi-Fi, and you'll likely also find it at tourist information offices, major museums, and public-transit hubs. With Wi-Fi you can use your phone or tablet to make free or inexpensive domestic and international calls via a calling app such as Skype, FaceTime, or Google+ Hangouts. When you can't find Wi-Fi, you can use your cellular network to connect to the Internet, text, or make voice calls. When you're done, avoid further charges by manually switching off "data roaming" or "cellular data."

It's possible to stay connected without a phone, but most **hotels** charge a fee for placing calls—ask for rates before you dial. You can use a prepaid international phone card—called a *cartão telefónico com código pessoal*—to call out from your hotel (available at post offices, newsstands, street kiosks, tobacco shops, and train stations). Dial the toll-free access number, enter the card's PIN code, then dial the number.

Public pay phones are getting harder to find. To use one, you'll need an insertable card called a *cartão telefónico*. These are

Sleep Code

Hotels are classified based on the average price of a standard double room with breakfast in high season.

$$$$	**Splurge:** Most rooms over €150
$$$	**Pricier:** €100-150
$$	**Moderate:** €70-100
$	**Budget:** €40-70
¢	**Backpacker:** Under €40
RS%	**Rick Steves discount**

Unless otherwise noted, credit cards are accepted, hotel staff speaks basic English, and free Wi-Fi is available. Comparison-shop by checking prices at several hotels (on each hotel's own website, on a booking site, or by email). For the best deal, *book directly with the hotel*. Ask for a discount if paying in cash; if the listing includes **RS%,** request a Rick Steves discount.

usable only at pay phones and provide reasonable rates for making calls within Portugal. They also work for international calls (though not as cheaply as international phone cards). Both types of phone cards work only in the country where you buy them.

For more on phoning, see www.ricksteves.com/phoning. For a one-hour talk on "Traveling with a Mobile Device," see www.ricksteves.com/travel-talks.

Sleeping

I've categorized my recommended accommodations based on price, indicated with a dollar-sign rating (see sidebar). In addition to standard hotels, I also list several simple, family-run hotels (listed as a *pensão* or *residencial*) and rooms in private homes (*quartos*) as budget alternatives. Portugal also has luxurious, government-sponsored historic inns (*pousadas*), which are full of Old World character but pricey.

Reserve rooms as soon as your itinerary is set. For the best rates, book directly with the hotel or B&B using their official website (not a booking agency's site). If there's no secure reservation form, or for complicated requests, send an email with the following information: number and type of rooms; number of nights; arrival date; departure date; and any special requests. Use the European style for writing dates: day/month/year. Hoteliers typically ask for your credit-card number as a deposit.

Some hotels are willing to make a deal to attract guests: Try emailing several hotels to ask their best price. In general, hotel prices can soften if you do any of the following: offer to pay cash, stay at least three nights, or travel off-season.

Restaurant Price Code

I've assigned each eatery a price category, based on the average cost of a typical main course. Drinks, desserts, and splurge items (steak and seafood) can raise the price considerably.

$$$$ **Splurge:** Most main courses over €17
$$$ **Pricier:** €12-17
$$ **Moderate:** €7-12
$ **Budget:** Under €7

In Portugal, takeout food is **$**; a basic sit-down eatery is **$$**; a casual but more upscale restaurant is **$$$**; and a swanky splurge is **$$$$**.

Eating

I've categorized my recommended eateries based on price, indicated with a dollar-sign rating (see sidebar). The Portuguese meal schedule is slightly later than in the US. Their breakfast *(pequeno almoço)* is often just coffee and a sweet roll. Lunch *(almoço)* is served between 12:30 and 14:00, while supper *(jantar)* is from about 19:30 to 21:30. All restaurants are smoke-free.

Eat fresh seafood in Portugal, except on Monday, when the fish isn't fresh. Cod *(bacalhau)* is a mainstay, but definitely an acquired taste. Fish soup *(sopa de peixe)* and shellfish soup *(sopa de mariscos)* are worth seeking out. Or, for a seafood blowout, look for *cataplana* (a feast from the sea, simmered in a copper pot). The "Portuguese paella" is *arroz de mariscos,* seafood stew with rice. *Carne de porco* á Alentejana is an interesting combination of pork and clams. *Caldo verde* is vegetable soup. *Frango assado* is roast chicken; ask for *piri-piri* sauce if you like it hot and spicy.

At a restaurant, be warned that if the waiter brings you an appetizer you didn't order (such as olives, bread, or pâtés), it isn't free. If you don't want it, push it to the side or ask the server to take it back—you won't be charged for what you don't touch. Eating just one olive means you pay for the whole dish.

Many restaurants save their customers money by portioning their dishes for two people. Menus often list prices for entrées in two columns: *dose* and *meia dose.* A *dose* is generally enough to feed two, while a *meia dose* is a half-portion (plenty for one person). Restaurants have absolutely no problem with diners splitting a single *dose. Prato do dia* is the daily special.

Tipping: When you want the bill, say, *"A conta, por favor."* At cafés and restaurants, a service charge is included in the price of what you order. If the service was good, it's customary to leave a tip of up to 5 percent—or 10 percent for a splurge place. Leave the tip on the table. It's best to tip in cash, even if you pay with your credit card. If you order your food at a counter, don't tip.

Transportation

By Bus and Train: Portugal straggles behind the rest of Europe in train service, but offers excellent bus transportation. Because of this, the country rail pass—the Portugal Pass—doesn't make much sense. The best public transportation option is to mix bus and train travel. Portugal has a number of different bus companies, sometimes running buses to the same destinations and using the same transfer points. If you have to transfer, make sure to look for a bus with the same name/logo as the company you bought the ticket from. The largest national company is Rede Expressos (covers buses both north and south of Lisbon, www.rede-expressos.pt).

To research train schedules, see Portugal's train website (www.cp.pt, includes Spain and France connections) or Germany's excellent all-Europe website (www.bahn.com). For information on rail passes, visit www.ricksteves.com/rail.

By Car: It's cheaper to arrange most car rentals from the US. For tips on your insurance options, see www.ricksteves.com/cdw, and for route planning, consult www.viamichelin.com. Bring your driver's license. If you're starting your trip in big-city Lisbon, don't rent a car until you're on your way out (and consider renting from the airport location). Note that it's simpler to day-trip to Sintra by train rather than by car.

Superhighways come with tolls, but save huge amounts of time if you're crossing the country. For some toll roads, you pick up a ticket as you enter. Other roads are tolled electronically using cameras, which identify cars by their license plate and charge the appropriate fees via a simple electronic payment system. To save some hassle paying tolls, rent a "Via Verde" automated toll sensor along with your car. Ask your car-rental agency about this toll system.

Be sure all of your valuables are out of sight and locked in the trunk, or even better, with you or in your hotel room. Local road etiquette is similar to that in the US. Ask your rental company about the rules of the road, or check the US State Department website (www.travel.state.gov, search for Portugal in the "Learn about your destination" box, then click on "Travel and Transportation").

Helpful Hints

Emergency Help: For English-speaking **police** or an **ambulance**, dial 112. For passport problems, call the **US Embassy** (in Lisbon—tel. 217-273-300, http://portugal.usembassy.gov).

If you have a minor illness, do as the locals do and go to a pharmacist for advice. Or ask at your hotel for help—they know of the nearest medical and emergency services. For other concerns, get advice from your hotelier.

Theft or Loss: While Lisbon is generally safe, if you're looking for trouble—especially after dark—you may find it. Pickpockets target tourists on popular trolley routes and the Metro. Don't believe any "police officers" looking for counterfeit bills. Enjoy the sightseeing, but be aware of your surroundings—wear your money belt.

To replace a passport, you'll need to go in person to an embassy (see above). Cancel and replace your credit and debit cards by calling these 24-hour US numbers collect: Visa—tel. 303/967-1096, MasterCard—tel. 636/722-7111, American Express—tel. 336/393-1111. In Portugal, to make a collect call to the US, dial 800-800-128; press zero or stay on the line for an operator. File a police report either on the spot or within a day or two; you'll need it to submit an insurance claim for lost or stolen rail passes or travel gear, and it can help with replacing your passport or credit and debit cards. For more information, see www.ricksteves.com/help.

Time: Portugal uses the 24-hour clock. It's the same through 12:00 noon, then keep going: 13:00, 14:00, and so on. Portugal's time zone is the same as Great Britain's: generally five/eight hours ahead of the East/West Coasts of the US.

Business Hours: Some businesses in Portugal take an afternoon break (usually 12:00-13:30 or 12:30-14:00). Small shops are often open on Saturday only in the morning and are closed all day Sunday. Banks are generally open Monday through Friday from 8:30 to 15:00.

Dress Code: At churches, a modest dress code (no bare shoulders or shorts) is encouraged.

Holidays and Festivals: Europe celebrates many holidays, which can close sights and attract crowds (book hotel rooms ahead). For information on holidays and festivals in Portugal, check the country's website: www.visitportugal.com. For a simple list showing major events, see www.ricksteves.com/festivals.

Numbers and Stumblers: What Americans call the second floor of a building is the first floor in Europe. Europeans write dates as day/month/year, so Christmas 2019 is 25/12/19. Commas are decimal points and vice versa—a dollar and a half is 1,50, and there are 5.280 feet in a mile. Portugal uses the metric system: A kilogram is 2.2 pounds; a liter is about a quart; and a kilometer is six-tenths of a mile.

Resources from Rick Steves

This Snapshot guide is excerpted from the latest edition of *Rick Steves Portugal*, which is one of many titles in my ever-expanding series of guidebooks on European travel. I also produce a public television series, *Rick Steves' Europe*, and a public radio show, *Travel with Rick Steves*. My website, www.ricksteves.com, offers free travel information, a forum for travelers' comments, guidebook updates, my travel blog, an online travel store, and information on European rail passes and our tours of Europe. If you're bringing a mobile device, my free Rick Steves Audio Europe app features podcasts of my radio shows, my free Lisbon City Walk audio tour, and travel interviews about Portugal. You can get Rick Steves Audio Europe via Apple's App Store, Google Play, or the Amazon Appstore. For more information, see www.ricksteves. com/audioeurope.

Additional Resources

Tourist Information: www.visitlisboa.com and www.visitportugal.com
Passports and Red Tape: www.travel.state.gov
Packing List: www.ricksteves.com/packing
Cheap Flights: www.kayak.com or www.google.com/flights
Airplane Carry-on Restrictions: www.tsa.gov/travelers
Updates for This Book: www.ricksteves.com/update

How Was Your Trip?

To share your tips, concerns, and discoveries after using this book, please fill out the survey at www.ricksteves.com/feedback. Thanks in advance—it helps a lot.

PRACTICALITIES

Portuguese Survival Phrases

In the phonetics, nasalized vowels are indicated by an underlined **n** or **w**. As you say the vowel, let its sound come through your nose as well as your mouth.

English	Portuguese	Pronunciation
Good day.	*Bom dia.*	boh<u>n</u> **dee**-ah
Do you speak English?	*Fala inglês?*	**fah**-lah een-**glaysh**
Yes. / No.	*Sim. / Não.*	seeng / no<u>w</u>
I (don't) understand.	*(Não) compreendo.*	(no<u>w</u>) koh<u>n</u>-pree-**ayn**-doo
Please.	*Por favor.*	poor fah-**vor**
Thank you. (said by male)	*Obrigado.*	oo-bree-**gah**-doo
Thank you. (said by female)	*Obrigada.*	oo-bree-**gah**-dah
I'm sorry.	*Desculpe.*	dish-**kool**-peh
Excuse me (to pass).	*Com licença.*	koh<u>n</u> li-**sehn**-sah
(No) problem.	*(Não) há problema.*	(no<u>w</u>) ah proo-**blay**-mah
Good.	*Bom.*	boh<u>n</u>
Goodbye.	*Adeus. / Ciao.*	ah-**deh**-oosh / chow
one / two	*um / dois*	oo<u>n</u> / doysh
three / four	*três / quatro*	traysh / **kwah**-troo
five / six	*cinco / seis*	**seeng**-koo / saysh
seven / eight	*sete / oito*	**seh**-teh / **oy**-too
nine / ten	*nove / dez*	**naw**-veh / dehsh
How much is it?	*Quanto é?*	**kwahn**-too eh
Write it?	*Escreva?*	ish-**kray**-vah
Is it free?	*É gratis?*	eh **grah**-teesh
Is it included?	*Está incluido?*	ish-**tah** een-kloo-**ee**-doo
Where can I find / buy...?	*Onde posso encontrar / comprar...?*	**ohn**-deh **paw**-soo ay<u>n</u>-koh<u>n</u>-**trar** / koh<u>n</u>-**prar**
I'd like / We'd like...	*Gostaria / Gostaríamos...*	goosh-tah-**ree**-ah / goosh-tah-**ree**-ah-moosh
...a room.	*...um quarto.*	oo<u>n</u> **kwar**-too
...a ticket to ___.	*...um bilhete para ___.*	oo<u>n</u> beel-**yeh**-teh **pah**-rah ___
Is it possible?	*É possível?*	eh poo-**see**-vehl
Where is...?	*Onde é que é...?*	**ohn**-deh eh keh eh
...the train station	*...a estação de comboio*	ah ish-tah-**sow** deh koh<u>n</u>-**boy**-yoo
...the bus station	*...a terminal de autocarros*	ah tehr-mee-**nahl** deh ow-too-**kah**-roosh
...the tourist information office	*...a posto de turismo*	ah **poh**-stoo deh too-**reez**-moo
...the toilet	*...a casa de banho*	ah **kah**-zah deh **bahn**-yoo
men	*homens*	**aw**-may<u>n</u>sh
women	*mulheres*	mool-**yeh**-rish
left / right	*esquerda / direita*	ish-**kehr**-dah / dee-**ray**-tah
straight	*em frente*	ay<u>n</u> **frayn**-teh
What time does this open / close?	*As que horas é que abre / fecha?*	ahsh keh **aw**-rahsh eh keh **ah**-breh / **feh**-shah
At what time?	*As que horas?*	ahsh keh **aw**-rahsh
Just a moment.	*Um momento.*	oo<u>n</u> moo-**mayn**-too
now / soon / later	*agora / em breve / mais tarde*	ah-**goh**-rah / ay<u>n</u> **bray**-veh / maish **tar**-deh
today / tomorrow	*hoje / amanhã*	**oh**-zheh / ah-ming-**yah**

PRACTICALITIES

In the Restaurant

English	Portuguese	Pronunciation
I'd like / We'd like...	Gostaria / Gostaríamos...	goosh-tah-**ree**-ah / goosh-tah-**ree**-ah-moosh
...to reserve...	...de reservar...	deh reh-zehr-**var**
...a table for one. / two.	...uma mesa para uma. / duas.	**oo**-mah **may**-zah **pah**-rah **oo**-mah / **doo**-ahsh
Non-smoking.	Não fumar.	no<u>w</u> foo-**mar**
Is this table free?	Esta mesa está livre?	ehsh-tah meh-zah ish-**tah** lee-vreh
The menu (in English), please.	A ementa (em inglês), por favor.	ah eh-**mayn**-tah (ay<u>n</u> een-**glaysh**) poor fah-vor
service (not) included	serviço (não) incluído	sehr-**vee**-soo (no<u>w</u>) een-kloo-ee-doo
cover charge	coberto	koh-**behr**-too
to go	para fora	**pah**-rah foh-rah
with / without	com / sem	koh<u>n</u> / say<u>n</u>
and / or	e / ou	ee / oh
specialty of the house	especialidade da casa	ish-peh-see-ah-lee-**dah**-deh dah **kah**-zah
half portion	meia dose	**may**-ah doh-zeh
daily special	prato do dia	**prah**-too doo **dee**-ah
tourist menu	ementa turística	eh-**mayn**-tah too-**reesh**-tee-kah
appetizers	entradas	ay<u>n</u>-**trah**-dahsh
bread / cheese	pão / queijo	pow / **kay**-zhoo
sandwich	sandes	**sahn**-desh
soup / salad	sopa / salada	**soh**-pah / sah-**lah**-dah
meat	carne	**kar**-neh
poultry	aves	**ah**-vish
fish / seafood	peixe / marisco	**pay**-shee / mah-**reesh**-koo
fruit	fruta	**froo**-tah
vegetables	legumes	lay-**goo**-mish
dessert	sobremesa	soo-breh-**may**-zah
tap water	água da torneira	**ah**-gwah dah tor-**nay**-rah
mineral water	água mineral	**ah**-gwah mee-neh-**rahl**
milk	leite	**lay**-teh
(orange) juice	sumo (de laranja)	**soo**-moo (deh lah-**rah**<u>n</u>-zhah)
coffee / tea	café / chá	kah-**feh** / shah
wine	vinho	**veen**-yoo
red / white	tinto / branco	**teen**-too / **brang**-koo
glass / bottle	copo / garrafa	**koh**-poo / gah-**rah**-fah
beer	cerveja	sehr-**vay**-zhah
Cheers!	Saúde!	sah-**oo**-deh
More. / Another.	Mais. / Outro.	maish / **oh**-troo
The same.	O mesmo.	oo **mehsh**-moo
The bill, please.	A conta, por favor.	ah-**kohn**-tah poor fah-**vor**
tip	gorjeta	gor-**zheh**-tah
Delicious!	Delicioso!	deh-lee-see-**oh**-zoo

For many more pages of survival phrases for your trip to Portugal, check out *Rick Steves' Portuguese Phrase Book & Dictionary.*

INDEX

Explore Europe

At ricksteves.com you can browse through thousands of articles, videos, photos and radio interviews, plus find a wealth of money-saving travel tips for planning your dream trip. And with our mobile-friendly website, you can easily access all this great travel information anywhere you go.

TV Shows

Preview the places you'll visit by watching entire half-hour episodes of Rick Steves' Europe (choose from all 100 shows) on-demand, for free.

your travel dreams into affordable reality

Radio Interviews

Enjoy ready access to Rick's vast library of radio interviews covering travel

tips and cultural insights that relate specifically to your Europe travel plans.

Travel Forums

Learn, ask, share! Our online community of savvy travelers is a great resource

for first-time travelers to Europe, as well as seasoned pros. You'll find forums on each country, plus travel tips and restaurant/hotel reviews. You can even ask one of our well-traveled staff to chime in with an opinion.

Travel News

Subscribe to our free Travel News e-newsletter, and get monthly updates from Rick on what's happening in Europe.

Rick's Free Travel App

Gear up for your next adventure at ricksteves.com

Light Luggage

Pack light and right with Rick Steves' affordable, custom-designed rolling carry-on bags, backpacks, day packs and shoulder bags.

Accessories

From packing cubes to moneybelts and beyond, Rick has personally selected the travel goodies that will help your trip go smoother.

Shop at ricksteves.com

Experience maximum Europe

Save time and energy

This guidebook is your independent-travel toolkit. But for all it delivers, it's still up to you to devote the time and energy it takes to manage the preparation and logistics that are essential for a happy trip. If that's a hassle, there's a solution.

Rick Steves Tours

A Rick Steves tour takes you to Europe's most interesting places with great

with minimum stress

guides and small groups of 28 or less. We follow Rick's favorite itineraries, ride in comfy buses, stay in family-run hotels, and bring you intimately close to the Europe you've traveled so far to see. Most importantly, we take away the logistical headaches so you can focus on the fun.

travelers—nearly half of them repeat customers—along with us on four dozen different itineraries, from Ireland to Italy to Istanbul. Is a Rick Steves tour the right fit for your travel dreams? Find out at ricksteves.com, where you can also request Rick's latest tour catalog. Europe is best experienced with happy travel partners. We hope you can join us.

Join the fun

This year we'll take thousands of free-spirited

Rick Steves

Nearly all Rick Steves guides are available as ebooks. Check with your favorite bookseller.

Rick Steves guidebooks are published by Avalon Travel, an imprint of Perseus Books, a Hachette Book Group company

Maximize your travel skills with a good guidebook.

Avalon Travel
An imprint of Perseus Books
A Hachette Book Group company
1700 Fourth Street
Berkeley, CA 94710

Text © 2017 by Rick Steves.
Maps © 2017 by Rick Steves' Europe.
Printed in Canada by Friesens. First printing July 2017.

For the latest on Rick's talks, guidebooks, Europe tours, public radio show, free
audio tours, and public television series, contact Rick Steves' Europe, 130 Fourth
Avenue North, Edmonds, WA 98020, tel. 425/771-8303, www.ricksteves.com,
rick@ricksteves.com.

ISBN 978-1-63121-621-3
3rd Edition

Rick Steves' Europe

Managing Editor: Jennifer Madison Davis
Special Publications Manager: Risa Laib
Editors: Glenn Eriksen, Tom Griffin, Katherine Gustafson, Suzanne Kotz, Cathy Lu,
    Carrie Shepherd
Editorial & Production Assistant: Jessica Shaw
Editorial Intern: Meesha Sundarum
Graphic Content Director: Sandra Hundacker
Maps & Graphics: David C. Hoerlein, Lauren Mills, Mary Rostad

Avalon Travel

Senior Editor and Series Manager: Madhu Prasher
Editor: Jamie Andrade
Associate Editor: Sierra Machado
Copy Editor: Kelly Lydick
Proofreader: Patty Mon
Indexer: Stephen Callahan
Production & Typesetting: Christine DeLorenzo, Rue Flaherty
Cover Design: Kimberly Glyder Design
Maps & Graphics: Kat Bennett, Mike Morgenfeld

Photo Credits

Front Cover: Rossio square in Lisbon © Mapics | Dreamstime.com
Title Page: Pena Palace in Sintra © Rui Vale de Sousa/123rf.com

Additional Photography: Dominic Arizona Bonuccelli, Reid Coen, Rich Earl,
Cameron Hewitt, David C. Hoerlein, Carol Ries, Jennifer Schutte, Robyn Stencil,
Rick Steves, Ashley Sytsma, Robert Wright, Wikimedia Commons—PD-Art/PD-US
(photos are used by permission and are the property of the original copyright owners)

ABOUT THE AUTHOR

RICK STEVES

 Since 1973, Rick has spent about four months a year exploring Europe. His mission: to empower Americans to have European trips that are fun, affordable, and culturally broadening. Rick produces a best-selling guidebook series, a public television series, and a public radio show, and organizes small-group tours that take over 20,000 travelers to Europe annually. He does all of this with the help of a hardworking, well-traveled staff of 100 at Rick Steves' Europe in Edmonds, Washington, near Seattle. When not on the road, Rick is active in his church and with advocacy groups focused on economic justice, drug policy reform, and ending hunger. To recharge, Rick plays piano, relaxes at his family cabin in the Cascade Mountains, and spends time with his partner Trish, son Andy, and daughter Jackie. Find out more about Rick at www.ricksteves.com and on Facebook.